PE[...]
GREEK[...]

D0481016

OTHER PENGUIN PHRASE BOOKS

Dutch
French
German
Italian
Portuguese
Spanish
Russian
Turkish

GREEK
PHRASE BOOK

THIRD EDITION

JILL NORMAN
NIKOS STANGOS

PENGUIN BOOKS

PENGUIN BOOKS

Published by the Penguin Group
27 Wrights Lane, London W8 5TZ, England
Viking Penguin Inc., 375 Hudson Street, New York, New York 10014, USA
Penguin Books Australia Ltd, Ringwood, Victoria, Australia
Penguin Books Canada Ltd, 2801 John Street, Markham, Ontario, Canada L3R 1B4
Penguin Books (NZ) Ltd, 182–190 Wairau Road, Auckland 10, New Zealand

Penguin Books Ltd, Registered Offices: Harmondsworth, Middlesex, England

First published in 1973
Second edition 1978
Third edition 1988
3 5 7 9 10 8 6 4

Filmset in Linotron 202 Ehrhardt by
Morton Word Processing Scarborough

Printed in England by Clays Ltd, St Ives plc

CONTENTS

INTRODUCTION

In this series of phrase books only those words and phrases that might be called essential to a traveller have been included, but the definition of 'traveller' has been made very wide, to include not only the business traveller and the holiday-maker, whether travelling alone, with a group or the family, but also the owner of a house, an apartment or a time-share. Each type of traveller has his or her own requirements, and for easy use the phrases are arranged in sections which deal with specific situations.

Pronunciation is given for each phrase and for all words in the extensive vocabulary. An explanation of the system used for the pronunciation guide is to be found on pages xii–xvi. It is essential to read this section carefully before starting to use the book.

Some of the Greek phrases are marked with an asterisk(*) – these attempt to give an indication of the kind of reply you might get to your question, and of questions you may be asked in your turn.

For those who would like to know a little more about the Greek language, a brief survey of the main points of its grammar is provided at the end of the book (pages 201–209).

PRONUNCIATION

The pronunciation guide is intended for people with no knowledge of modern Greek. As far as possible the system is based on English pronunciation. Each phrase and each word in the vocabulary is transliterated in Roman characters in accordance with this pronunciation guide. As a result, complete accuracy may sometimes be lost for the sake of simplicity, but if readers learn the Greek alphabet and the pronunciation of the letters, they should be able to understand modern Greek and make themselves understood.

THE ALPHABET

Modern Greek uses the same alphabet as ancient Greek and the spelling of words has remained virtually unchanged. Those who want to use or understand Greek must first learn the alphabet. In spite of the differences between English and Greek, this should not be difficult as most of the sounds are relatively easy to make.

The Greek alphabet has twenty-four letters.

capital	*lower case*	
Α	α	álpha (as **a** in dart)
Β	β	víta (as **v** in van)
Γ	γ	gháma (as y in yellow)
Δ	δ	dhélta (as **th** in this)
Ε	ε	épsilon (as **e** in let)
Ζ	ζ	zíta (as **z** in zone)
Η	η	íta (as **ee** in keep)
Θ	θ	thíta (as **th** in theatre)
Ι	ι	yióta (as **ee** in keep)
Κ	κ	kápa (as **k** in keep)
Λ	λ	lámda (as **l** in lemon)
Μ	μ	mi (as **m** in man)
Ν	ν	ni (as **n** in net)
Ξ	ξ	ksi (as **ks** in tracks)
Ο	ο	ómikron (as **o** in pot)
Π	π	pi (as **p** in past)
Ρ	ϱ	ro (as **r** in rain)
Σ	σ, ς[1]	síghma (as **s** in stone)
Τ	τ	taf (as **t** in time)
Υ	υ	ípsilon (as **ee** in keep)
Φ	φ	fi (as **f** in fan)
Χ	χ	hi (as **h** in hat)
Ψ	ψ	psi (as **ps** in eclipse)
Ω	ω	omégha (as **o** in home)

VOWELS

All vowels are pronounced distinctly; unstressed vowels keep their pure sound and are never slurred as in English. The letter **e** is always pronounced at the end of a word.

1. Only used at the end of a word.

(*Note:* Although lower case will be given mostly from now on, it is assumed that readers will be able to transfer to capitals once they have familiarized themselves with the letters of the alphabet.)

α, ε, η, ι, ο, υ, ω

πανί	pani (cloth)
λέξη	lexi (word)
ρήμα	rimma (verb)
μάτι	mati (eye)
στόμα	stoma (mouth)
φύλλο	filo (leaf)
φώς	fos (light)

COMPOUND VOWELS (DIPHTHONGS)

αι	as **e** in smell	παιδί	pedhi (child)
ει	as **ee** in keep	εἶμαι	ime (I am)
οι	as **ee** in keep	ὅλοι	oli (all)
ου	as **oo** in cool	πουλί	pooli (bird)
αυ	as **af** in after	αὐτόματος	aftomatos (automatic)
αυ	as **av** in avarice	αὔριο	avrio (tomorrow)
ευ	as **ef** in left	ἐλεύθερος	eleftheros (free)
ευ	as **ev** in seven	νεῦμα	nevma (sign)

CONSONANTS

β, γ, δ, ζ, θ, κ, λ, μ, ν, ξ, π, ρ, σ, τ, φ, χ, ψ

βάρκα	varka (boat)
γράμμα	gramma (letter)
δέντρο	dhendro (tree)
ζέστη	zesti (heat)
θέατρο	theatro (theatre)

καλός	kalos (good)
λίγο	ligho (a little)
μάτι	mati (eye)
νερό	nero (water)
ξανά	[1]xana (again)
πόδι	podhi (foot)
ρήμα	rima (verb)
στόμα	stoma (mouth)
τόπος	topos (place)
φώς	fos (light)
χέρι	heri (hand)
ψωμί	[1]psomi (bread)

GROUPS OF CONSONANTS

γγ	as **ng** in anger	αγγελία	angelia (notice)
γκ	as **g** in game at the beginning of a word	γκρεμος	gremos (precipice)
	as **ng** in singer within a word	μαραγκος	marangos (carpenter)
γξ	as **nx** in anxiety	φάλαγξ	falanx (phalanx)
γχ	as **nh**	εγχρωμος	enhromos (coloured)
μπ	as **b** in bare	μπότα	bota (boot)
μπ	as **mb** in member	λάμπα	lamba (lamp)
ντ	as **d** in dear	ντομάτα	domata (tomato)
ντ	as **nd** in end or **nt** in enter	δέντρο	dhendro (tree)
τζ	as **dz**	τζάκι	dzaki (fireplace)

STRESS

Unless written in capitals, almost all words (except for a few monosyllabic ones whose accent is absorbed by the word that precedes them) are

1. **x** and **ps** at the beginning of a word should be pronounced in the same way as in tracks or lips.

accented. Accents are indicated in this phrase book by **bold** type in the transliterations, and following recent practice in Greece, all accents are here reduced to ´. Vowels at the beginning of a word, whether in capitals or lower case, also bear breathings (ή, ἡ) which should be ignored. The diaeresis is used to separate vowels which otherwise would form a group. The diaeresis is indicated by αϊ as in παϊδι paidhi (rib) as compared to παιδί pedhi (child).

PUNCTUATION

The comma and full stop are used as in English. The Greek semicolon is a raised full stop (˙) and the question mark is like the English semicolon (;).

IDIOMS

There are two forms of modern Greek: the *dhemotiki* (demotic), which is the ordinary language spoken more or less throughout Greece (excepting the dialects); and the *katharevoussa* (purist), which, until recently, was mainly used for official documents, school and university text-books and sometimes in newspapers. The *katharevoussa* is an artificial form of Greek closer to older forms in the evolution of modern Greek from classical Greek. This phrase book uses the ordinary demotic language which most people speak. For this reason neologisms and foreign words which have entered the ordinary Greek vocabulary have not been excluded. On the contrary, where a word is identical or similar to an English one, and it is also common in Greek usage, we have deliberately chosen to use it in preference to a more traditional Greek word.

It is common in Greek to address people one does not know personally in the formal polite form rather than the familiar, which means using verbs in the second person plural. Almost all phrases in this book are constructed in the polite form.

ESSENTIALS

FIRST THINGS

Yes	**Ναί**	Ne
No	**Όχι**	Ohi
Please/you're welcome	**Παρακαλώ**	Parakalo
Thank you	**Ευχαριστώ**	Efharisto

LANGUAGE PROBLEMS

I'm English/American	**Είμαι Εγγλέζος/ Αμερικάνος**	Ime englezos/amerikanos
Do you speak English?	**Μιλάτε Αγγλικά;**	Milate anglika
Does anybody here speak English?	**Μιλάει κανείς αγγλικά εδώ;**	Milai kanis anglika edho
I don't speak Greek	**Δεν μιλώ Ελληνικά**	Dhen milao elinika

I speak a little Greek	Μιλώ λίγα Ελληνικά	Milao ligha elinika
Do you understand (me)?	(Με) καταλαβαίνετε;	(Me) katalavenete
I understand	Καταλαβαίνω	Katalaveno
I don't understand	Δεν καταλαβαίνω	Dhen katalaveno
Would you say that again, please?	Μπορείτε να επαναλάβετε παρακαλώ;	Borite na epanalavete parakalo
Please speak slowly	Μπορείτε να μιλήσετε πιο αργά σας παρακαλώ;	Borite na milissete pio argha sas parakalo
What does that mean?	Τι σημαίνει αυτό;	Ti simeni afto
Can you translate it for me?	Μπορείτε να μου το μεταφράσετε;	Borite na mou to metafrassete
Please write it down	Σας παρακαλώ γράψτε το	Sas parakalo ghrapste to
How do you say it in Greek?	Πως λέγεται στα Ελληνικά;	Pos leghete sta elinika
What do you call this in Greek?	Πως λέγεται στα Ελληνικά;	Pos leghete sta elinika
I don't speak (much) ...	Δεν μιλώ (πολλά) ...	Dhen milao (pola)
I will look it up in my phrase book	Θα το κοιτάξω στο βιβλιάριο των φράσεων μου	Tha to kitakso sto vivliario ton frasseon mou
Please show me the word in the book	Δείξτε μου σας παρακαλώ τη λέξη στο βιβλίο	Dhikste mou sas parakalo ti leksi sto vivlio

QUESTIONS

Who?	**Ποιός;**	Pios
Why?	**Γιατί;**	Ghiati
Where is/are ...?	**Που είναι ...;**	Pou ine
When?	**Πότε;**	Pote
How?	**Πώς;**	Pos
How much is/are ...?	**Πόσο κάνει/ κάνουν ...;**	Posso kani/kanoun
How much/many?	**Πόσο/πόσα;**	Posso/possa
How far?	**Πόσο μακριά;**	Posso makria
What's this?	**Τι είναι αυτό;**	Ti ine afto
What do you want?	**Τι θέλεις;**	Ti thelis
What must I do?	**Τι πρέπει να κάνω;**	Ti prepi na kano
Have you .../Do you sell ...?	**Έχετε ...;**	Ehete
Is there ...?	**Υπάρχει ...;**	Iparhi
Have you seen ...?	**Έχετε δει ...;**	Ehete dhi
May I have ...?	**Μπορώ να έχω ...;**	Boro na eho
I want/should like ...	**Θέλω/Θα ήθελα ...**	Thelo/tha ithela
I don't want ...	**Δεν θέλω**	Dhen thelo
What is the matter?	**Τι συμβαίνει;**	Ti simveni
Can you help me?	**Μπορείτε να με βοηθήσετε;**	Borite na me voithissete
Where can I find ...?	**Που μπορώ να βρω ...;**	Pou boro na vro
Have you seen ...?	**Είδατε ...;**	Idhate

| Can I help you? | *Μπορώ να σας βοηθήσω; | Boro na sas voithisso |
| Can you tell/give/show me ...? | Μπορείτε να μου πείτε/δώσετε/δείξετε ...; | Borite na mou pite/dhossete/dhiksete |

USEFUL STATEMENTS

Here is/are ...	Εδώ είναι ...	Edho ine
I like it/them	Μ'αρέσει/μ'αρέσουν	Maressi/maressoun
I don't like it/them	Δεν μ'αρέσει/ μ'αρέσουν	Dhen maressi/maressoun
I (don't) know	(Δεν) ξέρω	(Dhen) ksero
I didn't know	Δεν ήξερα	Dhen iksera
I think so	Νομίζω	Nomizo
I'm hungry	Πεινώ	Pinao
I'm thirsty	Διψώ	Dhipsao
I'm tired	Είμαι κουρασμένος	Ime kourasmenos
I'm in a hurry	Βιάζομαι	Viazome
I'm ready	Είμαι έτοιμος	Ime etimos
Leave me alone	Αφήστε με ήσυχο	Afiste me isiho
Just a minute	*Μια στιγμή	Mia stighmi
This way, please	*Απ'εδώ παρακαλώ	Apedho parakalo
Take a seat	*Καθίστε	Kathiste
Come in!	*Εμπρός	Embros
It's cheap	Είναι φθηνό	Ine fthino
It's (too) expensive	Είναι (πολύ) ακριβό	Ine (poli) akrivo

That's all	**Φτάνει**	Ftani
You're right	**Έχετε δίκιο**	Ehete dhikio
You're wrong	**Κάνετε λάθος**	Kanete lathos
It is ...	**Είναι ...**	Ine
It isn't ...	**Δεν είναι ...**	Dhen ine
I have ...	**Έχω ...**	Eho
I don't have ...	**Δεν έχω ...**	Dhen eho
I want ...	**Θέλω ...**	Thelo
I would like ...	**Θα ήθελα ...**	Tha ithela
I need ...	**Χρειάζομαι ...**	Hriazome
I'm lost	**Έχω χαθεί**	Eho hathi
We're looking for ...	**Ψάχνουμε ...**	Psahnoume
Here it is	**Νάτο**	Nato
There they are	**Νάτοι**	Nati
There is/are ...	**Είναι ...**	Ine
It's important	**Είναι σημαντικό**	Ine simantiko
It's urgent	**Είναι επείγον**	Ine epighon
You are mistaken	**Κάνετε λάθος**	Kanete lathos

GREETINGS

Good morning/good day	**Καλημέρα σας**	Kalimera sas
Good afternoon/ evening	**Καλησπέρα σας**	Kalispera sas
Good night	**Καληνύχτα σας**	Kalinihta sas

Hello	Γειά σας	Ghia sas
How are you?	Πως είσαστε;	Pos issaste
Very well, thank you	Πολύ καλά ευχαριστώ	Poli kala efharisto
Good-bye	Χαίρεται	Herete
See you tomorrow	Θα ιδωθούμε αύριο	Tha idhothoume avrio
Have a good journey	Καλό ταξίδι	Kalo taksidhi
Have a good time	Ελπίζω να περάσετε καλά	Elpizo na perassete kala
Good luck/all the best	Καλή τύχη/ότι επιθυμείτε	Kali tihi/oti epithimite

POLITE PHRASES

Sorry/excuse me	Συγγνώμη	Sighnomi
Excuse me	Με συγχωρήτε	Me sinhorite
That's all right	Δεν πειράζει	Dhen pirazi
Don't mention it/ you're welcome (*after thanks*)	Παρακαλώ	Parakalo
Don't worry	Μην ανησυχήτε	Min anissihite
It doesn't matter	Δεν πειράζει	Dhen pirazi
I beg your pardon?	Τι είπατε;	Ti ipate
Am I disturbing you?	Μήπως σας ενοχλώ;	Mipos sas enohlo
I'm sorry to have troubled you	Με συγχωρήτε για την ενόχληση	Me sinhorite ghia tin enohlissi
Everything all right?	Όλα εντάξει;	Ola entaksi

Good/that's fine	**Καλά/εντάξει**	Kala/entaksi
With pleasure	**Μετά χαράς**	Meta haras
Thank you for your trouble	**Σας ευχαριστώ για τον κόπο**	Sas efharisto ghia ton kopo
That's nice/beautiful	**Όμορφο/ωραίο**	Omorfo/oreo

OPPOSITES[1]

before/after	**πρίν/μετά**	prin/meta
early/late	**νωρίς/αργά**	noris/argha
first/last	**πρώτο/τελευταίο**	proto/telefteo
now/later, then	**τώρα/αργότερα, τότε**	tora/arghotera, tote
far/near	**μακριά/κοντά**	makria/konda
here/there	**εδώ/εκεί**	edho/eki
in/out	**μέσα/έξω**	messa/exo
inside/outside	**μέσα/έξω**	messa/exo
under/over	**από κάτω/από πάνω**	apo kato/apo pano
big, large/small	**μεγάλο/μικρό**	meghalo/mikro
deep/shallow	**βαθύ/ρηχό**	vathi/riho
empty/full	**άδειο/γεμάτο**	adhio/ghemato
fat/lean	**παχύ/αδύνατο**	pahi/adhinato
heavy/light	**βαρύ/ελαφρύ**	vari/elafri
high/low	**υψηλό/χαμηλό**	ipsilo/hamilo

1. All adjectives are given in their neuter form. The masculine form has the ending -os and the feminine -n or -a. See GRAMMAR pp. 201–209, for more information.

long, tall/short	μακρύ, υψηλό/χαμηλό	makri, ipsilo/hamilo
narrow/wide	στενό/πλατύ	steno/plati
thick/thin	χοντρό/λεπτό	hondro/lepto
least/most	λιγώτερο/περισσότερο	lighotero/perissotero
many/few	πολλά/λίγα	pola/ligha
more/less	περισσότερο/λιγώτερο	perissotero/lighotero
much/little	πολύ/λίγο	poli/ligho
beautiful/ugly	ωραίο/άσχημο	oreo/ashimo
better/worse	καλύτερο/χειρότερο	kalitero/hirotero
cheap/expensive	φθηνό/ακριβό	fthino/akrivo
clean/dirty	καθαρό/βρώμικο	katharo/vromiko
cold/hot, warm	κρύο/ζεστό, χλιαρό	krio/zesto, hliaro
easy/difficult	εύκολο/δύσκολο	efkolo/dhiskolo
fresh/stale	φρέσκο/μπαγιάτικο	fresko/baghiatiko
good/bad	καλό/κακό	kalo/kako
new, young/old	καινούργιο, νέο/παλιό	kenourghio, neo/palio
nice/nasty	καλό, συμπαθητικό/κακό, απαίσιο	kalo, simpathitiko/kako, apessio
occupied/vacant	πιασμένο/ελεύθερο	piasmeno/elelefthero
open/closed, shut	ανοικτό/κλειστό	anikto/klisto
quick/slow	γρήγορο/αργό	ghighoro/argho
quiet/noisy	ήσυχο/θορυβώδες	issiho/thorivodhes
right/wrong	σωστό/λανθασμένο	sosto/lanthasmeno
sharp/blunt	οξύ, κοφτερό/αμβλύ	oxi, koftero/amvli

SIGNS &
PUBLIC NOTICES[1]

Ανελκυστήρ/ασανσέρ	Lift/elevator
Ανοικτό	Open
Ανοίξατε από ... μέχρι ...	Open from ... to ...
Απαγορεύεται η είσοδος	No entry/no admission
Απαγορεύεται το κάπνισμα	No smoking
Αποχωρητήριο/τουαλέτα	Lavatory/toilet
Αστυνομία	Police station
Ενοικιάξεται δωμάτιο	Room to let
Είσοδος	Entrance
Είσοδος ελεύθερα	Admission free
Ελεύθερο	Vacant/free/unoccupied
Ενοικιάζεται	To let
Έξοδος (κινδύνου)	(Emergency) exit
Ιδιαίτερον	Private

1. See also TRAVEL (p. 19) and DRIVING (p. 40).

Κατειλημμένο	Engaged/occupied
Κίνδυνος	Danger
Κλειστό	Closed
Χτυπήστε τον κόδωνα	Ring
Κυρίων	Gentlemen
Κυριών/Γυναικών	Ladies
Μεταφραστής	Interpreter
Μη(ν) ...	Do not ...
Μη εγγίζετε	Do not touch
Μη πόσιμο νερό	Not for drinking
Μόνον όρθιοι	Standing room only
Οδηγός	Guide
Οι παραβάτες θα διωχθούν	Trespassers will be prosecuted
Όλο δεξιά	Keep right
Παρακαλείστε όπως μη ...	You are requested not to ...
Πεζοί	Pedestrians
Πιασμένο/Κατειλημμένο	Reserved
Πλήρες	House full (cinema, etc.)
Πληροφορείες	Information
Πόσιμο νερό	Drinking water
Πρός ενοικίαζεται	To let/for hire
Πρός πώλείται	For sale
Προσοχή	Caution
Πώλησις	Sale
Σύρατε	Pull
Ταμίας	Cashier

Ταχυδρομείο	Post office
Τράπεζα	Bank
Χώρος σταθμέυσεος αυτοκινήτων	Car park
Ωθήσατε	Push

MONEY[1]

Where is the nearest bank?	Που είναι η πλησιέστερη τράπεζα;	Pou ine i plissiesteri trapeza
Do you change travellers' cheques?	Αλλάζετε τράβελλερς τσέκς;	Allazete travellers' cheques
Where can I change travellers' cheques?	Που μπορώ ν'αλλάξω τράβελλερς τσέκς;	Pou boro nalaxo travellers' cheques
I want to change some pounds/dollars	Θέλω ν'αλλάξω μερικές λίρες/δολλάρια	Thelo nalaxo merikes lires/dholaria
How many drachmas to the pound/dollar?	Πόσες δραχμές στη λίρα/στο δολλάριο;	Posses dhrahmes sti lira/sto dholario
What is the rate of exchange?	Ποιά είναι η τιμή μεταλλαγής συναλλάγματος;	Pia ine i timi metalaghis sinalaghmatos

1. Banks are open from 8.00 to 13.00, Monday to Saturday, and some branches in Athens open in the afternoon during the tourist season.

Can you give me some small change, please?	**Μου δίνετε μερικά ψιλά παρακαλώ;**	Mou dhinete merika psila parakalo
Will you take a personal cheque?	**Παίρνετε προσωπικές επιταγές;**	pernete prossopikes epitaghes
Do you have any identification?	*Έχετε ταυτότητα;	Ehete taftotita
Sign here, please	*Υπογράψτε εδώ παρακαλώ	Ipoghrapste edho parakalo
Go to the cashier	*Πηγαίνετε στο ταμείο	Pighenete sto tamio
Please cash this Eurocheque	**Σας παρακαλώ αλλάξτε μου αυτό το Εύρωτσεχ**	Sas parakalo alakste mou afto to Evrotsek
Will you take a credit card?	**Παίρνετε κάρτες πιστώσεως;**	Pernete kartes pistoseos
I'd like to get some cash with my credit card	**Θέλω να τραβήξω λίγα χρήματα με την κάρτα πιστώθεως μου**	Thelo na traviko ligha hrimata me tin karta pistoseos mou
Where do I sign?	**Που να υπογράψω;**	Pou na ipoghrapso
I arranged for money to be transferred from England. Has it arrived yet?	**Έχω κανονίσει να μου σταλούν χρήματα από την Αγγλία. Έφτασαν;**	Eho kanonissi na mou staloun hrimata apo tin Anglia. Eftassan
I want to open a bank account	**Θέλω ν'ανοίξω ένα λογαριασμό**	Thelo naniko ena loghariasmo
Please credit this to my account	**Χρεώστε το στο λογαριασμό μου**	Hreoste to sto loghariasmo mou

Current account	**Τρεχούμενος λογαριασμός**	Trehoumenos loghariasmos
Deposit account	**Κατάθεση**	Katathessi
Statement	**Κίνηση λογαριασμού**	Kinissi loghariasmou
Balance	**Υπόλοιπο**	Ipolipo
Cheque book	**Βιβλιάριο επιταγών**	Vivliario epitaghon
Cheque card	**Κάρτα εξαργυρώσεως επιταγών**	Karta exarghirosseos epitaghon

CURRENCY

100 **Λεπτά** = 1 **Δραχμή**/pl. **Δραχμές**

100 lepta = 1 drahmi/pl. drahmes

TRAVEL

ARRIVAL

PASSPORT CONTROL AND CUSTOMS

Passport control	*Έλεγχος διαβατηρίων	Elenhos dhiavatirion
Your passport, please	*Το διαβατήριο σας παρακαλώ	To dhiavatirio sas parakalo
May I see your green card, please?	*Τα χαρτιά ασφαλείας σας παρακαλώ/την πράσινη κάρτα σας;	Ta hartia asfalias sas parakalo/tin prassini karta sas
Are you together?	*Είσαστε μαζί;	Issaste mazi
I'm travelling alone	Ταξιδεύω μόνος μου	Taksidhevo monos mou

I'm travelling with my wife/a friend	Ταξιδεύω με τη γυναίκα μου/ένα φίλο μου	Taksidhevo me ti ghineka mou/ena filo mou
I'm here on business/ on holiday	Έρχομαι γιά δουλειά/γιά διαχοπές	Erhome ghia dhoulia/ghia dhiakopes
What is your address in ...?	*Ποιά είναι η διεύθυνση σας στην ...;	Pia ine i dhiefthinssi sas stin
How long are you staying here?	*Πόσο θα μείνετε εδώ;	Posso tha minete edho
I have ...pounds/ dollars	Έχω ...λίρες/ δολλάρια	Eho ...lires/dholaria
Customs	*Τελωνείον	Telonion
Goods to declare	*Δηλωτέα αγαθά	Dhilotea aghatha
Nothing to declare	*Μηδέν πρός δήλωσιν	Midhen pros dhilossin
Which is your luggage?	*Ποιές είναι οι αποσκευές σας;	Pies ine i aposkeves sas
Do you have any more luggage?	*Έχετε άλλες αποσκευές;	Ehete ales aposkeves
This is (all) my luggage	Αυτές είναι (όλες) οι αποσκευές μου	Aftes ine (oles) i aposkeves mou
Have you anything to declare?	*Έχετε τίποτα να δηλώσετε;	Ehete tipota na dhilossete
You will have to pay duty on this	*Πρέπει να πληρώσετε φόρο γι'αυτό	Prepi na plirossete foro ghiafto

I have only my personal things in it	Έχω μόνο είδη προσωπικής χρήσεως	Eho mono idhi prossopikis hrisseos
I have a carton of cigarettes and a bottle of gin/wine	Έχω μία κούτα τσιγάρα κι'ένα μπουκάλι τζίν/κρασί	Eho mia kouta tsighara kiena boukali dsin/krassi
Open this bag, please	*Ανοίξτε αυτή τη βαλίτσα παρακαλώ	Anixte afti ti valitsa parakalo
Can I shut my case now?	Μπορώ να κλείσω τη βαλίτσα μου τώρα;	Boro na klisso ti valitsa mou tora
May I go?	Μπορώ να πηγαίνω;	Boro na pigheno

LUGGAGE

My luggage has not arrived	Οι αποσκευές μου δεν έφτασαν	I aposkeves mou dhen eftassan
My luggage is damaged	Οι αποσκευές μου είναι κατεστραμένες	I aposkeves mou ine katestramenes
One suitcase is missing	Λείπει μία βαλίτσα	Lipi mia valitsa
Are there any luggage trolleys?	Υπάρχουν καροτσάκια γιά βαλίτσες;	Iparhoun karotsakia ghia valitses
Where is the left luggage office?	Που είναι η αποθήκη αποσκευών;	Pou ine i apothiki aposkevon
Luggage lockers	Ντουλάπια αποσκευών	Doulapia aposkevon

Is there a bus/train into the centre?	Υπάρχει λεωφορείο/ τραίνο γιά το κέντρο;	Iparhi leoforio/treno ghia to kentro
How can I get to ...?	Πως θα πάω στο ...;	Pos tha pao sto
Where is the information bureau, please?	Που είναι το γραφείο πληροφοριών παρακαλώ;	Pou ine to ghrafio pliroforion parakalo
Porter!	Αχθοφόρε!	Ahthofore
Would you please take these bags to a taxi/ the bus?	Παίρνεις σε παρακαλώ αυτές τις βαλίτσες σ'ένα ταξί/στο λεωφορείο;	Pernis se parakalo aftes tis valitses sena taksi/ sto leoforio
What's the price for each piece of luggage?	Πόσα παίρνεις γιά κάθε βαλίτσα;	Possa pernis ghia kathe valitsa
I shall take this myself	Αυτό θα το κρατήσω	Afto tha to kratisso
That's not mine	Αυτό δεν είναι δικό μου	Afto dhen ine dhiko mou
Would you call a taxi?	Φωνάζεις ένα ταξί σε παρακαλώ;	Fonazis ena taksi se parakalo
How much do I owe you?	Πόσα σου οφείλω;	Possa sou ofilo

SIGNS TO LOOK FOR AT AIRPORTS AND STATIONS

Αφίξεις	Arrivals
Γραφείον εισιτηρίων	Booking office
Λεωφορεία	Buses
Ενοικίασις αντοκινήτων	Car rental
Ανταποκρίσεις	Connections
Αναχωρήσεις	Departures
Τράπεζα	Exchange/bank
Κυρίων	Gentlemen
Ξενοδοχεία	Hotels
Πληροφορίες	Information
Κυριών/Γυναικών	Ladies' room
Χαμένα αντικείμενα	Lost property
Αποσκευαί	Luggage
Θυρίδες αποσκευών	Luggage lockers
Κύριες γραμμές	Main lines
Εφημερίδες	Newspapers
Απαγορεύεται το κάπνισμα	Non-smoker
Πλατφόρμα	Platform
Αναψυκτικά	Refreshments
Κρατήσεις	Reservations
Επιτρέπεται το κάπνισμα	Smoker
Γραμμές περιχώρων	Suburban lines

Ταξί	Taxis
Εισιτήρια	Tickets
Τουριστικό γραφείο	Tourist office
Τράνζιτο	Transit
Ηλεκτρικό	Underground
Αίθουσα αναμονής	Waiting room

BUYING A TICKET

Where's the nearest travel agency?	Που είναι το πλησιέστερο γραφείο ταξιδιών;	Pou ine to plissiestero ghrafio taksidhion
Have you a timetable, please?	Έχετε ένα δρομολόγιο παρακαλώ;	Ehete ena dhromologhio parakalo
What's the tourist return fare to …?	Πόσο κάνει ένα εισιτήριο μετ'επιστροφής τουριστικής θέσεως γιά …;	Posso kani ena issitirio metepistrofis touristikis thesseos ghia
Is there a special rate for children?	Γίνεται ειδική τιμή γιά τα παιδιά;	Ghinete idhiki timi ghia ta pedhia
How old is he/she?	*Πόσο χρονό είναι;	Posso hrono ine
How much is it first class to …?	Πόσο στοιχίζει πρώτη θέση γιά …;	Posso stihizi proti thessi ghia
A second class ticket to …	Ένα εισιτήριο δευτέρας θέσεως γιά …	Ena issitirio dhefteras thesseos ghia

Three tickets to ...	Τρία εισιτήρια γιά ...	Tria issitiria ghia
Single/one way	Μονό/άνευ επιστροφής	Mono/anef epistrofis
A day return to ...	Ένα μετ'ἐπιστροφής γιά ...	Ena metepistrofis ghia
How long is this ticket valid?	Γιά πόσο ισχύει αυτό το εισιτήριο;	Ghia posso ishii afto to issitirio
Must I book in advance?	Είναι απαραίτητο να κλείσω θέση εκ των προτέρων;	Ine aparetito na klisso thessi ek ton proteron
Is there a cheaper midweek/weekend fare?	Υπάρχει φθηνότερο εισιτήριο στη μέση της εβδομάδας/το Σάββατο-Κύριακο;	Iparhi fthinotero issitirio sti messi tis evdhomadhas/to savatokiriako
When are you coming back?	*Πότε επιστρέφετε;	Pote epistrefete
Is there a cheaper day ticket?	Υπάρχει φθηνότερο εισιτήριο με επιστροφή αυθημερών;	Iparhi fthinotero issitirio me epistrofi afthimeron
Can I use it on the bus/underground too?	Μπορώ να το χρησιμοποιήσω και στο λεωφορείο/και στον ηλεκτρικό;	Boro na to hrissimopiisso ke sto leoforio/ke ston ilektriko

BY TRAIN

RESERVATIONS AND INQUIRIES

Where's the railway station?	Που είναι ο σιδηροδρομικός σταθμός;	Pou ine o sidhirodhromikos stathmos
Where is the ticket office?	Που είναι το εκδοτήριο των εισιτηρίων;	Pou ine to ekdhotirio ton issitirion
Two seats on the 11.15 tomorrow to ...	Δύο θέσεις γιά το τραίνο των ένδεκα και τέταρτο αύριο γιά ...	Dhio thessis ghia to treno ton endheka ke tetarto avrio ghia
I want to reserve a sleeper	Θέλω να κρατήσω μία κουκέττα	Thelo na kratisso mia kouketa
How much does a couchette cost?	Πόσο στοιχίζει η κουκέττα;	Posso stihizi i kouketa
I want to register this luggage through to ...	Θέλω να στείλω αυτές τις αποσκευές συστημένες στο ...	Thelo na stilo aftes tis aposkeves sistimenes sto
Is it an express or a local train?	Είναι ταχεία ή τοπικό τραίνο;	Ine tahia i topiko treno
Is there an earlier/later train?	Υπάρχει κανένα τραίνο πιό νωρίς/ αργότερα;	Iparhi kanena treno pio noris/arghotera
Is there a restaurant car on the train?	Υπάρχει εστιατόριο στο τραίνο;	Iparhi estiatorio sto treno

| I want a window seat/a corner seat/a seat in a non-smoking compartment | Θέλω μιά θέση στο παράθυρο/στη γωνία/σε χώρο μη καπνιστών | Thelo mia thessi sto parathiro/sti ghonia/se horo mi kapniston |
| When is the next train to …? | Πότε φεύγει το επόμενο τραίνο γιά …; | Pote fevghi to epomeno treno ghia |

CHANGING

Is there a through train to …?	Υπάρχει τραίνο κατ'ευθείαν γιά …;	Iparhi treno katefthian ghia
Do I have to change?	Πρέπει ν'αλλάξω;	Prepi nalakso
Where do I change?	Που πρέπει ν'αλλάξω;	Pou prepi nalakso
What time is there a connection to …?	Τί ώρα έχει ανταπόκριση γιά το …;	Ti ora ehi antapokrissi ghia to
Change at … and take the local train	Αλλάξτε στο … και πάρτε το τοπικό τραίνο	Alakste sto … ke parte to topiko treno

DEPARTURE

When does the train leave?	Πότε φεύγει το τραίνο;	Pote fevghi to treno
Which platform does the train to … leave from?	Από που φεύγει το τραίνο γιά το …;	Apo pou fevghi to treno ghia to …
Is this the train for …?	Είναι αυτό το τραίνο γιά το …;	Ine afto to treno ghia to

| There will be a delay of ... | *Έχει αργοπορία ... | Ehi arghoporia |
| Close the doors | *Κλείστε τις πόρτες | Kliste tis portes |

ARRIVAL

When does it get to ...?	Πότε φθάνει στο ...;	Pote fthani sto
Does the train stop at ...?	Σταματάει το τραίνο στο ...;	Stamatai to treno sto
Is the train late?	Έχει αργοπορία το τραίνο;	Ehi arghoporia to treno
When does the train from ... get in?	Τι ώρα φθάνει το τραίνο από ...;	Ti ora fthani to treno apo
At which platform?	Σε ποιά πλατφόρμα;	Se pia platforma
The train from ... is now arriving on platform ...	*Το τραίνο από το ... αφιχνείται στην πλατφόρμα ...	To treno apo to ... afiknite stin platforma

ON THE TRAIN

We have reserved seats	Έχουμε πιασμένες θέσεις	Ehoume piasmenes thessis
Is this seat free?	Είναι ελεύθερη αυτή η θέση;	Ine eleftheri afti i thessi
This seat is taken	Αυτή η θέση είναι πιασμένη	Afti i thessi ine piasmeni
Is this a smoking/ non-smoking compartment?	Είναι αυτό το βαγόνι γιά καπνιστές/γιά μη καπνιστές;	Ine afto to vaghoni ghia kapnistes/ghia mi kapnistes
Dining car	Βαγκόν-ρεστοράν	vakhon-restoran

Two tickets for lunch please	**Δύο εισιτήρια γιά φαγητό παρακαλώ**	Dhio issitiria ghia faghito parakalo
When does the buffet car open?	**Πότε ανοίγει το αναψυκτήριο;**	Pote anighi to anapsiktirio
Where is the sleeping car?	**Που είναι το βαγόνι με τις κουκέττες;**	Pou ine to vaghoni me tis kouketes
Which is my sleeper?	**Ποιά είναι η κουκέττα μου;**	Pia ine i kouketa mou
The heating is too high/too low	**Η θέρμανση είναι πολύ υψηλή/ χαμηλή**	I thermanssi ine poli ipsili/hamili
I can't open/close the window	**Δεν μπορώ ν'ανοίξω/να κλείσω το παράθυρο**	Dhen boro nanikso/na klisso to parathiro
What station is this?	**Ποιός σταθμός είναι αυτός;**	Pios stathmos ine aftos
How long do we stop here?	**Για πόσο θα σταματήσουμε εδώ;**	Ghia posso tha stamatissoume edho

BY AIR

Where's the Olympic office?	**Που είναι τα γραφεία της Ολυμπιακής;**	Pou ine ta ghrafia tis olimbiakis
I'd like to book two seats on the plane to ...	**Θέλω να κλείσω δύο θέσεις γιά το ...**	Thelo na klisso dhio thessis ghia to

Is there a flight to ...?	Υπάρχει πτήσις γιά το ...;	Iparhi ptissis ghia to
What is the flight number?	Ποιός είναι ο αριθμός πτήσεως;	Pios ine o arithmos ptisseos
When does it leave/ arrive?	Πότε φεύγει/φθάνει;	Pote fevghi/fthani
When does the next plane leave?	Πότε φεύγει το επόμενο αεροπλάνο;	Pote fevghi to epomeno aeroplano
Is there a coach to the airport/the town?	Υπάρχει λεωφορείο γιά το αεροδρόμιο/την πόλη;	Iparhi leoforio ghia to aerodhromio/tin poli
When must I check in?	Πότε πρέπει να παρουσιαστώ;	Pote prepi na paroussiasto
Please cancel my reservation to ...	Παρακαλώ ακυρώστε την κράτηση μου γιά ...	Parakalo akiroste tin kratissi mou ghia
I'd like to change my reservation to ...	Θέλω ν'αλλάξω την κράτηση μου γιά ...	Thelo nalakso tin kratissi mou ghia
I have an open ticket	Έχω ανοικτό εισιτήριο	Eho anikto issitirio
Can I change my ticket?	Μπορώ ν'αλλάξω το εισιτήριο μου;	Boro nalakso to issitirio mou
Will it cost more?	Θα στοιχίσει περισσότερο;	Tha stihissi perissotero

BY BOAT

Is there a boat/car ferry from here to ...?	Υπάρχει πλοίο/φέρρυ αυτοκινήτων απ'εδώ στο ...;	Iparhi plio/ferry aftokiniton apedho sto
How long does it take to get to ...?	Πόσο παίρνει να πάει κανείς στο ...;	Posso perni na pai kanis sto
How often do the boats leave?	Πόσο συχνά φεύγουν τα πλοία;	Poso sihna fevghoun ta plia
Where does the boat put in?	Που πιάνει το πλοίο;	Pou piani to plio
Does it call at ...?	Σταματάει στο ...;	Stamatai sto
When does the next boat leave?	Πότε φεύγει το επόμενο πλοίο;	Pote fevghi to epomeno plio
Can I book a single berth cabin?	Μπορώ να κλείσω μία μονή καμπίνα;	Boro na klisso mia moni kabina
How many berths are there in this cabin?	Πόσα κρεββάτια έχει αυτή η καμπίνα;	Possa krevatia ehi afti i kabina
When must we go on board?	Πότε πρέπει να επιβιβαστούμε;	Pote prepi na epivivastoume
When do we dock?	Πότε πλευρίζουμε;	Pote plevrizoume
How long do we stay in port?	Πόση ώρα θα μείνουμε στο λιμάνι;	Possi ora tha minoume sto limani
How do we get on to the deck?	Πως μπορούμε να πάμε στο κατάστρωμα;	Pos boroume na pame sto katastroma
Hydrofoil	Ιπτάμενο πλοίο	Iptameno plio
Lifebelt	Σωσίβιο	Sossivio

| Lifeboat | Σωσίβιος λέμβος | Sossivios lemvos |

BY UNDERGROUND

Where is the nearest underground station?	Που είναι ο πλησιέστερος σταθμός του ηλεκτρικό;	Pou ine o plissiesteros stathmos tou ilektriko
Which line goes to ...?	Ποιά γραμμή πηγαίνει στο ...;	Pia ghrami pigheni sto
Does this train go to ...?	Πηγαίνει αυτό το τραίνο στο ...;	Pigheni afto to treno sto
Where do I change for ...?	Που πρέπει ν'αλλάξω γιά το ...;	Pou prepi nalakso ghia to
Is the next station ...?	Είναι ο επόμενος σταθμός ο/η/το ...;	Ine o epomenos stathmos o/i/to
Which station is this?	Ποιός σταθμός είναι αυτός;	Pios stathmos ine aftos
Have you an underground map?	Έχετε χάρτη του ηλεκτρικό;	Ehete harti tou ilektriko

BY BUS OR COACH

Where's the bus station?	Που είναι ο σταθμός των λεωφορείων;	Pou ine o stathmos ton leoforion
Bus stop	*Στάσις λεωφορείου	Stassis leoforiou
When does the coach leave?	Πότε φεύγει το λεωφορείο;	Pote fevghi to leoforio

What time do we get to …?	Πότε φθάνουμε στο …;	Pote fthanoume sto
What stops does it make?	Που σταματάει;	Pou stamatai
Is it a long journey?	Είναι μακρύ ταξίδι;	Ine makri taxidhi
Is there a sightseeing tour?	Υπάρχει εκδρομή των αξιοθεάτων;	Iparhi ekdhromi ton aksiotheaton
What is the fare?	Πόσο κάνει το εισιτήριο;	Posso kani to issitirio
We want to make a sightseeing tour round the city	Θέλουμε να επισκεφτούμε τα αξιοθέατα της πόλης	Theloume na episkeftoume ta aksiotheata tis polis
Is there an excursion to … tomorrow?	Υπάρχει εκδρομή γιά το … αύριο;	Iparhi ekdhromi ghia to … avrio
Does the bus/coach stop at our hotel?	Σταματάει τό λεωφορείο/το πούλμαν στό ξενοδοχείο μας;	Stamatai to leoforio/to poulman sto ksenodhohio mas
What time is the next bus?	Πότε φεύγει τό επόμενο λεωφορείο;	Pote fevghi to epomeno leoforio
Has the last bus gone?	Πέρασε το τελευταίο λεωφορείο;	Perasse to telefteo leoforio
Does this bus go to the centre?	Πηγαίνει στο κέντρο αυτό το λεωφορείο;	Pigheni sto kentro afto to leoforio
Does this bus go to the beach?	Πηγαίνει αυτό το λεωφορείο στη παραλία;	Pigheni afto to leoforio sti paralia

Does this bus go to the station?	**Πηγαίνει αυτό το λεωφορείο στον σταθμό;**	Pigheni afto to leoforio ston stathmo
Does it go near ...?	**Πηγαίνει κοντά ...;**	Pigheni konta
Where can I get a bus to ...?	**Από που μπορώ να πάρω το λεωφορίο γιά ...;**	Apo pou boro na paro to leoforio ghia
I want to go to ...	**Θέλω να πάω στο ...**	Thelo na pao sto
Where do I get off?	**Που πρέπει να κατεύω;**	Pou prepi na katevo
Is this the right stop for ...?	**Είναι αυτή η σωστή στάση γιά το ...;**	Ine afti i sosti stassi ghia to
I want to get off at ...	**Θέλω να κατέβω στο ...**	Thelo na katevo sto
The bus to ... stops over there	***Το λεωφορείο γιά το ... σταματάει εκεί**	To leoforio ghia to ... stamatai eki
You must take a number ...	***Πρέπει να πάρετε το ...**	Prepi na parete to
You get off at the next stop	***Θα βγήτε στην επόμενη στάση**	Tha vghite stin epomeni stassi
The buses run every ten minutes/every hour	***Τα λεωφορεία περνούν κάθε δέκα λεπτά/κάθε ώρα**	Ta leoforia pernoun kathe dheka lepta/kathe ora

BY TAXI

Please get me a taxi	Μου φωνάζετε ένα ταξί σας παρακαλώ	Mou fonazete ena taksi sas parakalo
Where can I find a taxi?	Που μπορώ να βρω ένα ταξί;	Pou boro na vro ena taksi
Are you free?	Ελεύθερος;	Eleftheros
Please take me to Hotel Central/the station/this address	Μπορείς να με πας σε παρακαλώ στό Κεντρικό Ξενοδοχείο/στον σταθμό/σ'αυτή τη διεύθυνση	Boris na me pas se parakalo sto kentriko ksenodhohio/ston stathmo/safti ti dhiefthinssi
Can you hurry, I'm late?	Σε παρακαλώ κάνε γρήγορα γιατί έχω αργήσει;	Se parakalo kane ghrighora ghiati eho arghissi
Please wait a minute	Περίμενε σε παρακαλώ μιά στιγμή	Perimene se parakalo mia stighmi
Stop here	Σταμάτα εδώ	Stamata edho
Is it far?	Είναι μακριά;	ine makria
How far to ...?	Πόσο μακριά είναι το ...;	Posso makria ine to
Right/left at the next corner	Δεξιά/αριστερά στην άλλη γωνία	Dheksia/aristera stin ali ghonia
Straight on	Ίσια	Issia
How much do you charge for the hour/for the day?	Πόσα παίρνεις με την ώρα/τη μέρα;	Possa pernis me tin ora/ti mera

I'd like to go to … How much would you charge?	Θέλω να πάω στο … Πόσα θα πάρεις;	Thelo na pao sto … possa tha paris
How much is it?	Πόσο είναι;	Posso ine
That's too much	Είναι πάραπολυ	Ine parapoli
I am not prepared to spend that much	Δεν είμαι διατεθειμένος να ξοδέψω τόσα πολλά	Dhen ime dhiatethimenos na ksodhepso tossa pola
It's a lot, but all right	Πολλά είναι, αλλά εντάξει	Pola ine, ala endaksi

DIRECTIONS

Excuse me, could you tell me ...?	**Συγγνώμη, μου λέτε ...;**	Sighnomi, mou lete
Where is ...?	**Που είναι ...;**	Pou ine
Is this the way to ...?	**Αυτός είναι ο δρόμος γιά ...;**	Aftos ine o dhromos ghia
Which is the road for ...?	**Ποιός είναι ο δρόμος γιά ...;**	Pios ine o dhromos ghia
Is this the right road for ...?	**Αυτός είναι ο σωστός δρόμος γιά το ...;**	Aftos ine o sostos dhromos ghia to
How far is the next village/the next petrol station?	**Πόσο απέχει το επόμενο χωριό/ο επόμενος σταθμός βενζίνης;**	Posso apehi to epomeno horio/o epomenos stathmos venzinis
How far is it to ...?	**Πόσο απέχει ...;**	Posso apehi
How many kilometres?	**Πόσα χιλιόμετρα;**	Possa hiliometra

We want to get on to the motorway to ...	Θέλουμε να πάρουμε τον αυτοκινητόδρομο γιά ...	Theloume na paroume ton aftokinitodhromo ghia
Which is the best road to ...?	Ποιός ειναι ο καλύτερος δρόμος γιά ...;	Pios ine o kaliteros dhromos ghia
Is there a scenic route to ...?	Υπάρχει κανένας γραφικός δρόμος γιά ...;	Iparhi kanenas ghrafikos dhromos ghia
Where does this road lead to?	Που οδηγεί αυτός ο δρόμος;	Pou odhighi aftos o dhromos
Is it a good road?	Είναι καλός δρόμος;	Ine kalos dhromos
Is it a motorway?	Είναι αυτοκινητόδρομος;	Ine aftokinitodhromos
Is there a toll?	Έχει διόδια;	Ehi dhiodhia
Is the tunnel open/the pass open?	Είναι το τούνελ ανοιχτό/η διάβαση ανοιχτή;	Ine to tounel anikto/i dhiavassi anikti
Is the road to ... clear?	Είναι ο δρόμος γιά το ... ελεύθερος;	Ine o dhromos ghia to ... eleftheros
How long will it take by car/by bicycle/on foot?	Πόσο παίρνει με τ'αυτοκίνητο/το ποδήλατο/τα πόδια;	Posso perni me taftokinito/to podhilato/ta podhia
Will we get to ... by evening?	Θα φθάσουμε στο ... μέχρι το βράδυ;	Tha fthassoume sto ... mehri to vradhi
Where are we now?	Που είμαστε τώρα;	Pou imaste tora
What is the name of this place?	Πως ονομάζεται αυτό το μέρος;	Pos onomazete afto to meros

Please show me on the map	Δείξτε μου σας παρακαλώ στόν χάρτη	Dhikste mou sas parakalo ston harti
One-way system	Μονή κατεύθυνση	Moni katefthinssi
North	Βορράς	Voras
South	Νότος	Notos
East	Ανατολή	Anatoli
West	Δύση	Dhissi
It's that way	*Είναι απ'εδώ	Ine apedho
It isn't far	*Δεν είναι μακριά	Dhen ine makria
Follow this road for 5 kilometres	*Ακολουθήστε αυτό τον δρόμο γιά πέντε χιλιόμετρα	Akolouthiste afto to dhromo ghia pente hiliometra
Follow signs for ...	*Ακολουθήστε τις πινακίδες γιά το ...	Akolouthiste tis pinakidhes ghia to
Keep straight on	*Προχωρήστε ίσια	Prohoriste issia
Turn right at the crossroads	*Στρίψτε δεξιά στο σταυροδρόμι	Stripste dheksia sto stavrodhromi
Take the second road on the left	*Πάρτε τον δεύτερο δρόμο αριστερά	Parte ton dheftero dhromo aristera
Turn right at the traffic-lights	*Στρίψτε δεξιά στα φώτα κυκλοφορίας	Stripste dheksia sta fota kikloforias
Turn left after the bridge	*Στρίψτε αριστερά μετά τη γέφυρα	Stripste aristera meta ti ghefira
You are going the wrong way	*Έχετε πάρει λάθος δρόμο	Ehete pari lathos dhromo

| The best road is the ... | *Ο καλύτερος δρόμος είναι ... | O kaliteros dhromos ine |
| Take this road as far as ... and ask again | *Πάρτε αυτόν τον δρόμο μέχρι ... και ξαναρωτήστε | Parte afton ton dhromo mehri ... ke ksanarotiste |

DRIVING

GENERAL

Where is the nearest car park/nearest garage?	Που είναι ο πλησιέστερος χώρος σταθμεύσεως/το πλησιέστερο γκαράζ;	Pou ine o plissiesteros horos stathmefseos/to plissiestero garaz
Can I park here?	Μπορώ να παρκάρω εδώ;	Boro na parkaro edho
How long can I park here?	Πόση ώρα μπορώ να παρκάρω εδώ;	Possi ora boro na parkaro edho
No parking	*Απαγορεύεται η στάθμευσις	Apaghorevete i stathmefsis
Have you any change for the meter please?	Έχετε παρακαλώ ψιλά γιά το ρολόι σταθμεύσεως;	Ehete parakalo psila ghia to roloi stathmefseos

Speed limit	**Ανώτατο όριο ταχύτητος**	Anotato orio tahititos
Pedestrian precinct	**Πεζόδρομος**	Pezodhromos
Is this your car?	***Είναι δικό σας αυτό τό αυτοκίνητο;**	Ine dhiko sas afto to aftokinito
May I see your licence, please?	***Μπορώ να δω την άδεια οδηγήσεως σας παρακαλώ;**	Boro na dho tin adhia odhighiseos sas parakalo
How far is the next petrol station?	**Πόσο απέχει ο επόμενος σταθμός βενζίνης;**	Posso apehi o epomenos stathmos venzinis
Do you have a road map of ...?	**Έχετε έναν οδικό χάρτη του ...;**	Ehete enan odhiko harti tou

CAR HIRE

Where can I hire a car?	**Που μπορώ να νοικιάσω ένα αυτοκίνητο;**	Pou boro na nikiasso ena aftokinito
I want to hire an automatic	**Θέλω να νοικιάσω ένα αυτόματο**	Thelo na nikiasso ena aftomato
I need it for two days/a week	**Το χρειάζομαι γιά δύο μέρες/μία εβδομάδα**	To hriazome ghia dhio meres/mia evdhomadha
How much is it by the hour/day/week?	**Πόσο κάνει την ώρα/μέρα/ εβδομάδα;**	Posso kani tin ora/mera/ evdhomadha
Does that include mileage?	**Συμπεριλαμβάνονται σ'αυτό τα χιλιόμετρα;**	Simberilamvanonte safto ta hiliometra

Is there a weekend rate/a midweek rate?	Έχετε ειδική ταρίφα γιά τα Σαββατοκύριακα/το μέσο της εβδομάδας;	Ehete idhiki tarifa ghia ta savatokiriaka/to messo tis evdhomadhas
Do you want a deposit?	Θέλετε προκαταβολή;	Thelete prokatavoli
I will pay by credit card	Θα πληρώσω με πιστωτική κάρτα	Tha plirosso me pistotiki karta
The charge per kilometre is ...	*Η τιμή κατά χιλιόμετρο είναι ...	I timi kata hiliometro ine
Do you want full insurance?	*Θέλετε πλήρη ασφάλιση;	Thelete pliri asfalissi
I want the collision waiver, but not personal accident cover	Θέλω αντιπαροχή σε περίπτωση συγκρούσεως, αλλά όχι γιά την κάλυψη προσωπικού ατυχήματος	Thelo antiparohi se periptossi singrousseos, ala ohi ghia tin kalipsi prossopikou atihimatos
May I see your driving licence?	*Μπορώ να δω την άδεια οδηγήσεως σας;	Boro na dho tin adhia odhighisseos sas
Can I return it to your office in ...?	Μπορώ να το επιστρέψω στο γραφείο σας στο ...;	Boro na to epistrepso sto ghrafio sas sto
Could you show me the controls/lights, please?	Μου δείχνετε το σύστημα χειρισμού της μηχανής/των φώτων παρακαλώ;	Mou dhihnete to sistima hirismou tis mihanis/ ton foton parakalo

ROAD SIGNS

Αδιέξοδος	Dead end
Ανάψατε τά φώτα/τους προβολείς	Lights on/use headlights
Ανώμαλη/ολισθηρή επιφάνεια	Uneven/slippery surface
Απαγορεύεται η είσοδος	No entry
Απαγορεύεται η προσπέρασις	Overtaking prohibited
Απαγορεύεται η στάθμευσις	No parking
Απότομος λόφος	Steep hill
Αργά	Slow
Αργή κυκλοφορία	Slow traffic
Βαρέα οχήματα	Heavy vehicles
Διά πεζούς μόνον	Pedestrians only
Δρόμος κλειστός	Road blocked/closed
Εκχείλισις	Flooding
Επίπεδος διάβασις	Level crossing
Επιτρέπεται η στάθμευσις	Parking allowed
Ευθεία	Get in lane/straight on
Έξοδος φορτηγών αυτοκινήτων	Exit for lorries
Καμπή	Curves/bend
Κατευθείαν κυκλοφορία	Through traffic
Κίνδυνος	Danger
Κλειστή οδός	Road closed
Λωρίς λεωφορείων	Bus lane
Με δίσκους σταθμεύσεως	Parking discs required
Μονόδρομος	One way street

Μπείτε στην λωρίδα κυκλοφορίας οχυμάτων	Get in lane
Οδηγήτε με προσοχή	Drive with care
Οδικά έργα	Road works ahead
Ολισθηρή επιφάνεια	Slippery surface
Όλο δεξιά	Keep right
Όριον ταχύτητος	Speed limit
Παρέκκλισις	Diversion
Περιορισμένη στάθμευσις	Restricted parking
Προσοχή	Caution/attention
Προσωρινή επίστρωση	Temporary road surface
Πτώσις βράχων	Falling rocks
Σταματήστε	Stop
Στροφές	Winding road
Τελωνείον	Customs
Τέλος ζώνης απαγορευμένης σταθμεύσεως	End of no-parking zone
Φώτα οδικής κυκλοφορίας	Traffic lights

AT THE GARAGE OR PETROL STATION

Fill it up	**Γεμιστε το**	Ghemiste to
How much is petrol a litre?	**Πόσο κάνει το λίτρο η βενζίνη;**	Posso kani to litro i venzini
... litres of petrol, please	**... λίτρα βενζίνης παρακαλώ**	... litra venzinis parakalo

... (money's worth) of petrol, please	... δραχμές βενζίνης παρακαλώ	... dhrahmes venzinis parakalo
Please check the battery the brakes the oil the transmission fluid	Παρακαλώ κοιτάξτε τη μπαταρία τα φρένα το λάδι τα υγρά του κινωτίου ταχυτήτων	Parakalo kitaxte ti bataria ta frena to ladhi ta ighra tou kinotiou tahititon
the tyre pressure, including the spare	την πίεση στα λάστιχα, και της ρεζέρβας	tin piessi sta lastiha, ke tis rezervas
the water	το νερό	to nero
The oil needs changing	Το λάδι θέλει άλλαγμα	To ladhi theli alaghma
Check the tyre pressure, please	Κοιτάξτε τον αέρα στα λάστιχα παρακαλώ	Kitaxte ton aera sta lastiha parakalo
Please change the tyre	Αλλάξτε το λάστιχο παρακαλω	Alakste to lastiho parakalo
Would you clean the windscreen, please?	Καθαρίζεις τα τζάμια σε παρακαλώ;	Katharizis ta dzamia se parakalo
Please wash the car	Παρακαλώ πλύντε τ'αυτοκίνητο	Parakalo plinte taftokinito
Can I garage the car here?	Μπορώ να βάλλω τ'αυτοκίνητο σ'αυτό εδώ το γκαράζ;	Boro na valo taftokinito safto edho to garaz
What time does the garage close?	Τι ώρα κλείνει το γκαράζ;	Ti ora klini to garaz

| Where are the toilets? | Που είναι τα τουαλέτα; | Pou ine ta toualeta |

REPAIRS

My car's broken down	Χάλασε τ'αυτοκίνητο μου	Halasse taftokinito mou
Can I use your phone?	Μπορώ να χρησιμοποιήσω το τηλέφωνο σας;	Boro na hrissimopiisso to tilefono sas
Can you give me a lift to a telephone?	Μπορείτε να με πάτε κάπου που να'χει τηλέφωνο;	Borite na me pate kapou pou nahi tilefono
Please tell the next garage to send help	Σας παρακαλώ πέστε στο επόμενο γκαράζ να στείλει βοήθεια	Sas parakalo peste sto epomeno garaz na stili voithia
Where is there an ... agency?	Που είναι η αντιπροσωπεία των ...;	Pou ine i antiprossopia ton
Have you a breakdown service?	Κάνετε διορθώσεις;	Kanete dhiorthossis
Is there a mechanic?	Υπάρχει μηχανικός;	Iparhi mihanikos
Can you send someone to look at it/tow it away?	Μπορείτε να στείλετε κάποιον να το κοιτάξει/να το ρυμουλκήσει;	Borite na stilete kapion na to kitaxi/na to rimoulkissi
It is an automatic and cannot be towed	Είναι αυτόματο και δεν μπορεί να ρυμουλκηθεί	Ine aftomato ke dhen bori na rimoulkithi

Where are you/is your car?	*Που βρίσκεσται/ βρίσκεται τ'αυτοκίνητο σας;	Pou vriskeste/vriskete taftokinito sas
I am on the road from ... to ... near kilometre post ...	Είμαι στον δρόμο που πηγαίνει από το ... στο ... κοντά στο χιλιομετρικό πόστο ...	Ime ston dhromo pou pigheni apo to ... sto ... konta sto hiliometriko posto ...
I want the car serviced	Θέλω να μου κάνετε συντήρηση του αυτοκινήτου	Thelo na mou kanete sintirissi tou aftokinitou
This tyre is punctured	Αυτό το λάστιχο τρύπησε	Afto to lastiho tripisse
The valve is leaking	Η βαλβίδα τρέχει	I valvidha trehi
The battery is flat, it needs charging	Η μπαταρία είναι άδεια, θέλει γέμισμα	I bataria ine adhia, theli ghemisma
I've lost my car key	Έχασα το κλειδί του αυτοκίνητου μου	Ehassa to klidhi tou aftokinitou mou
The exhaust is broken	Είναι σπασμένη η εξάτμιση	Ine spasmeni i eksatmissi
The windscreen wipers do not work	Δεν λειτουργούν οι καθαριστήρες του παρμπρίς	Dhen litourghoun i katharistires tou parbriz
The lock is broken/ jammed	Η κλειδαριά είναι σπασμένη/κόλλησε	I klidharia ine spasmeni/ kolisse
My car won't start	Δεν ξεκινάει τ'αυτοκίνητο μου	Dhen ksekinai taftokinito mou
It's not running properly	Δεν λειτουργεί κανονικά	Dhen litourghi kanonika

The engine is overheating	Παραζεσταίνεται η μηχανή	Parazestenete i mihani
The engine is firing badly	Η μηχανή δεν τραβάει	I mihani dhen travai
Can you change this plug?	Μπορείτε ν'αλλάξετε αυτή τη βαλβίδα;	Borite n'alaksete afti ti valvidha
There's a petrol/oil leak	Τρέχει η βενζίνη/το λάδι	Trehi i venzini/to ladhi
There's a smell of petrol/rubber	Μυρίζει βενζίνη/ λάστιχο	Mirizi venzini/lastiho
The radiator is blocked/leaking	Το καλοριφέρ είναι βουλωμένο/τρέχει	To kalorifer ine voulomeno/trehi
Something is wrong with	Κάτι έχει (sing.)/ έχουν (pl.)	Kati ehi/ehoun
the brakes	τα φρένα	ta frena
my car	τ'αυτοκίνητο μου	taftokinito mou
the clutch	ο συμπλέκτης	o simplektis
the engine	η μηχανή	i mihani
the gearbox	οι ταχύτητες	i tahitites
the lights	τα φώτα	ta fota
the steering	το τιμόνι	to timoni
There's a whine/ rumble/rattle	Κάνει ένα θόρυβο/ μία βοή/ένα κρότο	Kani ena thorivo/mia voi/ena kroto
It's a high/low noise	Είναι ένας οξύς/ χαμηλός θόρυβος	Ine enas oksis/hamilos thorivos
It's intermittent/ continuous	Είναι διαχεκομμένος/ συνεχής	Ine dhiakekomenos/ sinehis
The carburettor needs adjusting	Το καρμπιρατέρ πρέπει να ρυθμιστεί	To karbirater prepi na rithmisti

Can you repair it?	Μπορείτε να το διορθώσετε;	Borite na to dhiorthossete
How long will it take to repair?	Πόσο θα σας πάρει να το διορθώσετε;	Posso tha sas pari na to dhiorthossete
What will it cost?	Τι θα στοιχίσει;	Ti tha stihissi
When can I pick the car up?	Πότε μπορώ να πάρω τ'αυτοκίνητο;	Pote boro na paro taftokinito
I need it as soon as possible	Το χρειάζομαι όσο το δυνατόν συντομώτερα	To hriazome osso to dhinaton sintomotera
I need it in three hours/tomorrow morning	Το χρειάζομαι σε τρεις ώρες/αύριο το πρωί	To hriazome se tris ores/avrio to proi
It will take two days	*Θα πάρει δύο μέρες	Tha pari dhio meres
We can repair it temporarily	*Μπορούμε να το επιδιορθώσουμε προσωρινά	Boroume na to epidhiorthossoume prossorina
We haven't the right spares	*Δεν έχουμε τα κατάλληλα ανταλλακτικά	Dhen ehoume ta katalila antalaktika
We have to send for the spares	*Πρέπει να παραγγείλουμε τ'ανταλλακτικά	Prepi na parangiloume tantalaktika
You will need a new ...	*Χρειάζεστε ένα καινούργιο ...	Hriazeste ena kenourghio
Could I have an itemized bill, please?	Μπορώ να έχω έναν αναλυτικό λογαριασμό παρακαλώ;	Boro na eho enan analitiko loghariazmo parakalo

PARTS OF A CAR AND OTHER USEFUL WORDS

accelerate (to)	πατώ το γκάζι	pato to gazi
accelerator	γκάζι	gazi
air pump	αεραντλία	aerandlia
alignment	ένωση	enossi
alternator	εναλλακτήρ	enalaktir
anti-freeze	αντιψυκτικό	antipsiktiko
automatic transmission	αυτόματη μεταλλαγή	aftomati metalaghi
axle	άξων τροχού	axon trohou
axleshaft	ακτίνα άξονος	aktina aksonos
battery	μπαταρία	bataria
beam	ακτίνα	aktina
bonnet/hood	καπώ	kapo
boot/trunk	πόρτ μπαγκάζ	port bagaz
brake	φρένο	freno
disc brakes/drum brakes	δισκόφρενα/ αερόφρενα	dhiskofrena/aerofrena
footbrake/handbrake	ποδόφρενο/ χειρόφρενο	podhofreno/hirofreno
brake fluid/lights	υγρό/φώτα φρένων	ighro/fota frenon
brake lining/pads	επένδυσις τακάκια φρένων	ependhissis takakia frenon
bulb	λαμπτήρ	lamptir
bumper	προφυλακτήρ	profilaktir

carburettor	καρμπιρατέρ	karbirater
carwash	πλύσιμο	plissimo
choke	βαλβίδα αέρος καρμπιρατέρ	valvidha aeros karbirater
clutch	συμπλέκτης	simplektis
clutch plate	δίσκος συμπλέκτου	dhiskos simplektou
coil	σύρμα	sirma
condenser	συμπυκνωτής	simpiknotis
cooling system	σύστημα ψύξεως	sistima psikseos
crankshaft	μανιβέλλα	manivela
cylinder	κύλινδρος	kilindhros
differential gear	διαφορική ταχύτης	dhiaforiki tahitis
dip stick	λαδόμετρο	ladhometro
distilled water	απεσταγμένο νερό	apestaghmeno nero
distributor	διανομεύς	dhianomefs
door	πόρτα	porta
doorhandle	χερούλι	herouli
drive (to)	οδηγώ	odhigho
driver	οδηγός	odhighos
dynamo	δυναμό	dhinamo
electrical trouble	ηλεκτρική βλάβη	ilektriki vlavi
engine	μηχανή	mihani
exhaust	εξάτμιση	eksatmissi
fan	ανεμιστήρας	anemistiras
fanbelt	λουρίδα ανεμιστήρος	louridha anemistiros
(oil) filter	φίλτρο (λαδιού)	filtro (ladhiou)

foglamp	φως ομίχλης	fos omihlis
fusebox	ασφάλειες	asfalies
gear	ταχύτης	tahitis
gear box/lever	κιβώτιο/μοχλός ταχυτήτων	kivotio/mohlos tahititon
grease (to)	γρασάρω	ghrassaro
headlights	προβολείς	provolis
heater	καλοριφέρ	kalorifer
horn	κλάξον	klakson
hose	λάστιχο	lastiho
ignition	μίζα	miza
ignition coil/key	σύρμα/κλειδί μίζας	sirma/klidhi mizas
indicator	δείκτης	dhiktis
jack	γερανός	gheranos
lights	φώτα	fota
lock/catch	κλειδαριά	klidharia
mechanical trouble	μηχανική βλάβη	mihaniki vlavi
mirror	καθρέπτης	kathreptis
number (plate)	αριθμός	arithmos
oil	λάδι	ladhi
oil pressure	πίεση λαδιού	piessi ladhiou
overdrive	υπερθέρμανση	iperthermanssi
parking lights	φώτα σταθμεύσεως	fota stathmefseos
petrol	βενζίνη	venzini
petrol can	δοχείον βενζίνης	dhohion venzinis
petrol pump/tank	αντλία/ντεπόζιτο βενζίνης	antlia/depozito venzinis

piston	πιστόνι	pistoni
piston ring	δακτύλιος πιστονιού	dhaktilios pistoniou
plug spanner	διωστήρ μπουζί	dhiostir bouzi
points	σημεία επαφής πλατινών	simia epafis platinon
propeller shaft	άξων	akson
(fuel/water) pump	αντλία (βενζίνης/νερού)	antlia (venzinis/nerou)
puncture	τρύπημα λαστίχου	tripima lastihou
radiator	ψυγείω	psighion
rear axle/lights	πίσω άξονας/φώτα	pisso aksonas/fota
reverse (to)	κάνω όπισθεν	kano opisthen
reverse	όπισθεν	opisthen
reversing lights	φώτα της όπισθεν	fota tis opisthen
(sliding) roof	σκεπή (συρτή)	skepi (sirti)
roof-rack	σχάρα	skhara
screwdriver	κατσαβίδι	katsavidhi
seat	θέση	thessi
shock absorber	σουσπανσιόν	souspansion
sidelights	πλαϊνά φώτα	plaina fota
silencer	κατασιγαστής	katassighastis
spanner	κλειδί	klidhi
spares	ανταλλακτικά	antalaktika
sparking plug	μπουζί	bouzi
speed	ταχύτης	tahitis
speedometer	δείκτης ταχύτητος	dhiktis tahititos
spring	ελατήριο	elatirio

stall (to)	σταματώ	stamato
starter	μίζα	miza
steering	οδήγησις	odhighissis
steering wheel	τιμόνι	timoni
sunroof	καπώ	kapo
suspension	ανάρτησις	anartissis
switch	διακόπτης	dhiakoptis
tank	ντεπόζιτο	depozito
tappets	μπουλόνια	boulonia
transmission	μεταφορά	metafora
tyre	λάστιχο	lastiho
tyre pressure	πίεσις λαστίχου	piessis lastihou
valve	βαλβίδα	valvidha
wheel	τροχός	trohos
wheels	ρόδες	rodhes
back	πίσω	pisso
front	μπρός	bros
spare	ρεζέρβα	rezerva
window	παράθυρο	parathiro
windscreen	παρμπρίζ	parbriz
windscreen washers/	πλυντήρες/	plindires/katharistires
wipers	καθαριστήρες	parbriz
	παρμπρίζ	
wing	φτερό	ftero

CYCLING

Where can I hire a bicycle?	Που μπορώ να νοικιάσω ένα ποδήλατο;	Pou boro na nikiasso ena podhilato
Do you have a bicycle with gears?	Έχετε ένα ποδήλατο με ταχύτητες;	Ehete ena podhilato me tahitites
The saddle is too high/too low	Η σέλα είναι πολύ ψηλά/χαμηλά	I sela ine poli psila/hamila
Where is the cycle shop?	Που είναι το μαγαζί ποδηλάτων;	Pou ine to maghazi podhilaton
Do you repair bicycles?	Επιδιορθώνετε ποδήλατα;	Epidhiorthonete podhilata
The brake isn't working	Δεν δουλεύει το φρένο	Dhen dhoulevi to freno
Could you tighten/loosen the brake cable?	Μπορείτε να σφίξετε/χαλαρώσετε το καλώδιο του φρένου;	Borite na sfiksete/halarossete to kalodhio tou frenou

A spoke is broken	Έχει σπάσει μιά ακτίνα	Ehi spassi mia aktina
The tyre is punctured	Έχει τρυπήσει το λάστιχο	Ehi tripissi to lastiho
The gears need adjusting	Οι ταχύτητες χρειάζονται ρύθμιση	I tahitites hriazonte rithmissi
Could you straighten the wheel?	Μπορείτε να ισιώσετε τη ρόδα;	Borite na issiossete ti rodha
The handlebars are loose	Το τιμόνι είναι χαλαρό	To timoni ine halaro
Could you please lend me a spanner/a tyre lever?	Σας παρακαλώ μπορείτε να μου δανείσετε ένα κλειδί/ένα λεβιέ γιά το λάστιχο;	Sas parakalo borite na mou dhanissete ena klidhi/ena levie ghia to lastiho

PARTS OF A BICYCLE

axle	άξονας	aksonas
bell	κουδούνι	koudhouni
brake	φρένο	freno
front	μπρός	bros
rear	πίσω	pisso
brake cable	καλώδιο φρένου	kalodhio frenou
brake lever	χερούλι φρένου	herouli frenou
bulb	λάμπα	lamba
chain	αλυσίδα	alissidha
dynamo	δυναμό	dhinamo

frame	σκελετός	skeletos
gear lever	μωχλός ταχυτήτων	mohlos tahititon
gears	ταχύτητες	tahitites
handlebars	τιμόνι	timoni
inner tube	σαμπρέλα	sabrela
light	φως	fos
front	μπρός	bros
rear	πίσω	pisso
mudguard	προφυλακτήρας λάσπης	profilaktiras laspis
panniers	καλάθια	kalathia
pedal	πεντάλι	pedhali
pump	τρόμπα	tromba
reflector	αντανακλαστήρας	andhanaklastiras
rim	ζάντα	zandha
saddle	σέλα	sela
saddlebag	θήκη σέλας	thiki selas
spoke	ακτίνα	aktina
tyre	λάστιχο	lastiho
valve	βαλβίδα	valvidha
wheel	ρόδα	rodha

HOTELS & GUEST HOUSES

BOOKING A ROOM

Rooms to let	*Ενοικιάζονται δωμάτια	Enikiazonte dhomatia
No vacancies	*Πλήρες	Plires
Receptionist	Υπάλληλος υποδοχής	Ipalilos ipodhohis
Have you a room for the night?	Έχετε ένα δωμάτιο γιά απόψε;	Ehete ena dhomatio ghia apopse
I've reserved a room. My name is ...	Έχω κρατήσει ένα δωμάτιο. Ονομάζομαι ...	Eho kratissi ena dhomatio. Onomazome
Can you suggest another hotel?	Ξέρετε κανένα άλλο ξενοδοχείο;	Kserete kanena alo ksenodhohio
I want a single room with a shower/a private toilet	Θέλω ένα μονό δωμάτιο με ντους/ ιδιωτική τουαλέτα	Thelo ena mono dhomatio me douz/ idhiotiki toualeta

We want a room with a double bed and a bathroom	Θέλουμε ένα δωμάτιο μ'ένα διπλό κρεββάτι καί μπάνιο	Theloume ena dhomatio mena dhiplo krevati ke banio
Have you a room with twin beds?	Έχετε ένα δωμάτιο με δύο κρεββάτια;	Ehete ena dhomatio me dhio krevatia
How long will you be staying?	*Πόσο θα μείνετε;	Posso tha minete
Is it for one night only?	*Είναι γιά μία μόνο νύχτα;	Ine ghia mia mono nikta
I want a room	Θέλω ένα δωμάτιο	Thelo ena dhomatio
for two or three days	γιά δύο ή τρεις μέρες	ghia dhio i tris meres
for a week	γιά μία εβδομάδα	ghia mia evdhomadha
until Friday	ώς τη Παρασκευή	os ti paraskevi
What floor is the room on?	Σε ποιό πάτωμα είναι το δωμάτιο;	Se pio patoma ine to dhomatio
Is there a lift/elevator?	Έχει ασανσέρ;	Ehi assansser
Have you a room on the first floor?	Έχετε ένα δωμάτιο στο πρώτο πάτωμα;	Ehete ena dhomatio sto proto patoma
May I see the room?	Μπορώ να δω το δωμάτιο;	Boro na dho to dhomatio
I like this room. I'll take it	Μ'αρέσει αυτό το δωμάτιο. Θα το πάρω	Maressi afto to dhomatio. Tha to paro
I don't like this room	Δεν μ'αρέσει αυτό το δωμάτιο	Dhen maressi afto to dhomatio
Have you another one?	Έχετε κανένα άλλο;	Ehete kanena alo

I want a quiet room/a bigger room	Θέλω ένα ήσυχο δωμάτιο/ένα μεγαλύτερο δωμάτιο	Thelo ena issiho dhomatio/ena meghalitero dhomatio
There's too much noise	Έχει πολύ θόρυβο	Ehi poli thorivo
I'd like a room with a balcony	Θα ήθελα ένα δωμάτιο με μπαλκόνι	Tha ithela ena dhomatio me balkoni
Have you a room looking on to the street/sea?	Έχετε ένα δωμάτιο που να βλέπει στο δρόμο/στη θάλασσα;	Ehete ena dhomatio pou na vlepi sto dhromo/sti thalassa
Is there a telephone/radio/television in the room?	Έχει τηλέφωνο/ραδιόφωνο/τηλεόραση στο δωμάτιο;	Ehi tilefono/radhiofono/tileorassi sto dhomatio
We've only a double room	*Έχουμε μόνο διπλό δωμάτιο	Ehoume mono dhiplo dhomatio
This is the only room vacant	*Αυτό είναι το μόνο άδειο δωμάτιο	Afto ine to mono adhio dhomatio
We shall have another room tomorrow	*Θα έχουμε ένα άλλο δωμάτιο αύριο	Tha ehoume ena alo dhomatio avrio
The room is only available tonight	*Το δωμάτιο είναι ελεύθερο μόνον απόψε	To dhomatio ine elesthero monon apopse
How much is the room per night?	Πόσο κάνει το δωμάτιο τη νύχτα;	Posso kani to dhomatio ti nihta
What is the price per week?	Πόσο κάνει κατά εβδομάδα;	Posso kani kata evdhomadha
It's too expensive	Είναι πολύ ακριβό	Ine poli akrivo

Have you nothing cheaper?	Δεν έχετε τίποτα πιό φθηνό;	Dhen ehete tipota pio fthino
Are service and tax included?	Συμπεριλαμβάνεται η υπηρεσία και ο φόρος;	Simperilamvanete i ipiressia ke o foros
How much is the room without meals?	Πόσο κάνει το δωμάτιο χωρίς γεύματα;	Posso kani to dhomatio horis ghevmata
How much is full board/half board?	Πόσο κάνει με όλα τα γεύματα/μόνο ένα;	Posso kani me ola ta ghevmata/mono ena
Is breakfast included in the price?	Συμπεριλαμβάνεται το πρόγευμα στη τιμή;	Simperilamvanete to proghevma sti timi
What do we pay for the child(ren)?	Πόσο θα πληρώσουμε γιά το παιδί/τα παιδιά;	Posso tha plirossoume ghia /to pedhi/ta pedhia
Could you put a cot/an extra bed in the room, please?	Μπορείτε να βάλετε ένα κρεββατάκι/ ένα επιπλέον κρεββάτι στο δωμάτιο παρακαλώ;	Borite na valete ena krevataki/ena epipleon krevati sto dhomatio parakalo
Would you fill in the registration form, please?	*Συμπληρώνετε την φόρμα εγγραφής παρακαλώ;	Simblironete tin forma enghrafis parakalo
Could I have your passport, please?	*Μου δίνετε το διαβατήριο σας παρακαλώ;	Mou dhinete to dhiavatirio sas parakalo
Are there facilities for the disabled?	Παρέχετε διευκολύνσεις γιά τους αναπήρους;	Parehete dhiefkolinssis ghia tous anapirous

IN YOUR ROOM

Chambermaid	Καμαριέρα	Kamariera
Room service	Υπηρεσία δωματίου	Ipiressia dhomatiou
Could we have breakfast in our room, please?	Μπορούμε να έχουμε πρόγευμα στο δωμάτιο μας παρακαλώ;	Boroume na ehoume proghevma sto dhomatio mas parakalo
I'd like some ice cubes	Θέλω λίγα παγάκια	Thelo ligha paghakia
There's no ashtray in my room	Δεν υπάρχει τασάκι στο δωμάτιο μου	Dhen iparhi tasaki sto dhomatio mou
Can I have more hangers, please?	Μπορώ να έχω περισσότερες κρεμάστρες σας παρακαλώ;	Boro na eho perissoteres kremastres sas parakalo
Is there a point for an electric razor?	Έχει πρίζα γιά ηλεκτρική ξυριστική μηχανή;	Ehi priza ghia ilektriki ksiristiki mihani
What's the voltage?[1]	Πόσα βολτ είναι το ρεύμα;	Possa volt ine to revma
Where is the bathroom/the lavatory?	Που είναι το μπάνιο/το αποχωρητήριο;	Pou ine to banio/to apohoritirio
Is there a shower?	Έχει ντους;	Ehi douz
There are no towels in my room	Δεν έχει πετσέτες στο δωμάτιο μου	Dhen ehi petsetes sto dhomatio mou

1. In Athens and most parts of the mainland the voltage is 220 d.c. On some of the islands it is 110 d.c.

There's no soap	Δεν έχει σαπούνι	Dhen ehi sapouni
There's no (hot) water	Δεν έχει (ζεστό) νερό	Dhen ehi (zesto) nero
There's no plug in my washbasin	Ο νυπτήρας μου δεν έχει βούλωμα	O niptiras mou dhen ehi vouloma
There's no toilet paper in the lavatory	Δεν έχεί χαρτί στο αποχωρητήριο	Dhen ehi harti sto apohoritirio
The lavatory won't flush	Δεν τρέχει το νερό στο αποχωρητήριο	Dhen trehi to nero sto apohoritirio
The bidet leaks	Ο μπιντές τρέχει	O bides trehi
The light doesn't work	Το φώς δεν λειτουργεί	To fos dhen litourghi
The lamp is broken	Η λάμπα είναι σπασμένη	I lamba ine spasmeni
The blind is stuck	Το παντζούρι έχει κολλήσει	To pandzouri ehi kolissi
The curtains won't close	Οι κουρτίνες δεν κλείνουν	I kourtines dhen klinoun
May I have the key to the bathroom, please?	Μου δίνετε το κλειδί του μπάνιου παρακαλώ;	Mou dhinete to klidhi tou baniou parakalo
May I have another blanket/another pillow?	Μου δίνετε άλλη μιά κουβέρτα/άλλο ένα μαξιλλάρι;	Mou dhinete ali mia kouverta/alo ena maksilari
These sheets are dirty	Αυτά τα σεντόνια είναι βρώμικα	Afta ta sendonia ine vromika
I can't open the window. Please open it for me.	Δεν μπορώ ν'ανοίξω το παράθυρο. Μου το ανοίγετε σας παρακαλω	Dhen boro nanikso to parathiro. Mou tanighete sas parakalo

It's too hot/cold	**Κάνει πολλή ζέστη/ κρύο**	Kani poli zesti/krio
Can the heating be turned up/turned down/turned off?	**Μπορείτε να ανεβάσετε/να χαμηλώσετε/να σβύσετε τη θέρμανση;**	Borite nanevassete/na hamilossete/na svissete ti thermanssi
Is the room air-conditioned?	**Έχει το δωμάτιο κλιματισμός;**	Ehi to dhomatio klimatismos
The air conditioning doesn't work	**Το κλιματισμός δεν λειτουργεί**	To klimatismos dhen litourghi
Come in!	**Εμπρός**	Embros
Put it on the table, please	**Αφίστετο στο τραπέζι παρακαλώ**	Afisteto sto trapezi parakalo
Would you clean these shoes, please?	**Μου καθαρίζετε αυτά τα παπούτσια παρακαλώ;**	Mou katharizete afta ta papoutsia parakalo
Would you clean this dress, please?	**Μου καθαρίζετε αυτό το φόρεμα σας παρακαλώ;**	Mou katharizete afto to forema sas parakalo
Would you press this suit, please?	**Μου σιδερώνετε αυτή τη φορεσιά παρακαλώ;**	Mou sidheronete afti ti foressia parakalo
How long will the laundry take?	**Πόση ώρα θα πάρει γιά να πλυθούν τα ρούχα;**	Possi ora tha pari ghia na plithoun ta rouha
Have you a needle and thread?	**Έχετε κλωστή και βελόνα;**	Ehete klosti ke velona
When will it be ready?	**Πότε θα είναι έτοιμο;**	Pote tha ine etimo

| It will be ready tomorrow | ***Θα είναι έτοιμο αύριο** | Tha ine etimo avrio |

OTHER SERVICES

Porter	**Πορτιέρης**	Portieris
Hall porter	**Πορτιέρης υποδοχής**	Portieris ipodhohis
Manager	**Διευθυντής**	Dhiefthindis
Telephonist	**Τηλεφωνητής** (m asc.)/ **τηλεφωνήτρια** (fem .)	Tilefonitis/tilefonitria
My key, please	**Το κλειδί μου παρακαλώ**	To klidhi mou parakalo
Can I leave this in your safe?	**Μπορώ να τ'αφίσω αυτό στο χρηματοκιβώτιο σας;**	Boro na tafisso afto sto hrimatokivotio sas
I'd like a map of the town/an amusement guide	**Θέλω ένα χάρτη της πόλης/οδηγό ψυχαγωγίας**	Thelo ena harti tis polis/ odhigho psihaghoghias
Are there any letters for me?	**Έχω γράμματα;**	Eho ghrammata
Are there any messages for me?	**Έχω τίποτα μηνύματα;**	Eho tipota minimata
Please post this	**Παρακαλώ ταχυδρομήστε μου αυτό**	Parakalo tahidhromiste mou afto
Is there a telex?	**Έχετε τήλεξ;**	Ehete tileks

Can I dial direct to England/America?	Μπορώ να πάρω κατ'ευθείαν Αγγλία/Αμερική;	Boro na paro katefthian anglia/ameriki
If anyone phones, tell them I'll be back at 4.30	Αν τηλεφωνήσει κανείς, να πείτε πως θα επιστρέψω στις τεσσερισήμιση	An tilefonissi kanis, na pite pos tha epistrepso stis tesserissimissi
No one telephoned	*Δεν τηλεφώνησε κανείς	Dhen tilefonisse kanis
There's a lady/ gentleman to see you	*Ένας κύριος/μία κυρία θέλει να σας δει	Enas kirios/mia kiria theli na sas dhi
Please ask her/him to come up	Πέστε της/του να έρθει επάνω	Peste tis/tou na erthi epano
I'm coming down	Κατεβαίνω	Kateveno
Have you any writing paper?	Έχετε χαρτί επιστολογραφίας;	Ehete harti epistologhrafias
envelopes? stamps?	φακέλλους; γραμματόσημα;	fakelous ghramatossima
Can I borrow a typewriter?	Μπορώ να δανειστώ μιά γραφομηχανή;	Boro na dhanisto mia ghrafomihani
Please send the chambermaid/the waiter	Στείλτε παρακαλώ την καμαριέρα/τον σερβιτόρο	Stilte parakalo tin kamariera/ton servitoro
I need a guide/an interpreter	Χρειάζομαι έναν οδηγό/διερμηνέα	Hriazome enan odhigho/dhierminea
Does this hotel have a baby-sitter service?	Έχει αυτό το ξενοδοχείο υπηρεσία γιά μπέϊμπισιτερ;	Ehi afto to ksenodhohio ipiressia ghia baby-sitter

Where are the toilets/ the cloakroom?	Που είναι οι τουαλέτες/η γκαρνταρόμπα;	Pou ine i toualetes/i gardaroba
Where is the dining room?	Που είναι η τραπεζαρία;	Pou ine i trapezaria
What time is breakfast? lunch? dinner?	Τι ώρα είναι το πρόγευμα; μεσημεριανό; βραδινό;	Ti ora ine to proghevma messimeriano vradhino
Is there a garage?	Υπάρχει γκαράζ;	Iparhi garaz
Where can I park the car?	Που μπορώ να παρκάρω το αυτοκίνητο;	Pou boro na parkaro to aftokinito
Is the hotel open all night?	Είναι ανοικτό το ξενοδοχείο όλο το βράδυ;	Ine anikto to ksenodhohio olo to vradhi
What time does it close?	Τι ώρα κλείνει;	Ti ora klini
Please wake me at ...	Ξυπνήστε με σας παρακαλώ στις ...	Ksipniste me sas parakalo stis

DEPARTURE

| I have to leave tomorrow | Πρέπει να φύγω αύριο | Prepi na figho avrio |
| Can you have my bill ready? | Μου ετοιμάζετε το λογαριασμό μου παρακαλώ; | Mou etimazete to logharasmo mou parakalo |

Can we check out at ...?	Μπορούμε να αναχωρήσουμε στις ...;	Boroume na anahorissoume stis
Do you accept credit cards?	Δέχεστε κάρτες πιστώσεως;	Dheheste kartes pistoseos
There is a mistake on the bill	Ο λογαριασμός έχει ένα λάθος	O loghariasmos ehi ena lathos
I shall be coming back on ...; can I book a room for that date?	Θα επιστρέψω στις .... μπορώ να κλείσω ένα δωμάτιο γι'αυτή την ημερομηνία;	Tha epistrepso stis ... boro na klisso ena dhomatio ghiafti tin imerominia
Could you have my luggage brought down?	Λέτε να μου φέρουν κάτω τις αποσκευές μου;	Lete na mou feroun kato tis aposkeves mou
Please store the luggage, we will be back at ...	Σας παρακαλώ αποθηκέψτε τις βαλίτσες, θα γυρίσουμε στις ...	Sas parakalo apothikepste tis valitses, tha ghirissoume stis
Please call a taxi for me	Φωνάξτε ένα ταξί σας παρακαλώ	Fonakste ena taksi sas parakalo
Thank you for a pleasant stay	Ευχαριστώ γιά την ευχάριστη διαμονή	Efharisto ghia tin efharisti dhiamoni

CAMPING

Is there a camp site nearby?	Υπάρχει τόπος κατασκηνώσεως εδώ κοντά;	Iparhi topos kataskinosseos edho konda
May we camp	Μπορούμε να κατασκηνώσουμε	Boroume na kataskinossoume
here?	εδώ;	edho
in your field?	στο χωράφι σας;	sto horafi sas
on the beach?	στη παραλία;	sti paralia
Where should we put our tent?	Που να στήσουμε τη σκηνή μας;	Pou na stissoume ti skini mas
Can I park the car next to the tent?	Μπορώ να παρκάρω τ'αυτοκίνητο δίπλα στη σκηνή;	Boro na parkaro taftokinito dhipla sti skini
Can we hire a tent?	Μπορούμε να νοικιάσουμε μια σκηνή;	Boroume na nikiassoume mia skini
Is/are there	Έχει	Ehi
drinking water?	πόσιμο νερό;	possimo nero
electricity?	ηλεκτρικό;	ilektriko

showers?	ντους;	douz
toilets?	τουαλέτες;	toualetes
What does it cost	Πόσο κάνει	Posso kani
per night?	τη νύχτα;	ti nihta
per week?	την εβδομάδα;	tin evdhomadha
per person?	κατ'άτομο;	katatomo
Is there	Έχει	Ehi
a shop	μαγαζί	maghazi
a swimming pool	πισίνα	pissina
a playground	παιδική χαρά	pedhiki hara
a restaurant	εστιατόριο	estiatorio
a launderette	πλυντήριο κατασκηνώσεως	plindirio kataskinosseos
on the site?	στο χώρο;	sto horo
Can I buy ice?	Μπορώ ν'αγοράσω πάγο;	Boro naghorasso pagho
Where can I buy paraffin/butane gas?	Που μπορώ ν'αγοράσω πετρέλαιο/γκάζι;	Pou boro naghorasso petreleo/gazi
Where do I put rubbish?	Που ρίχνουν τα σκουπίδια;	Pou rihnoun ta skoupidhia
Where can I wash up/ wash clothes?	Που μπορώ να πλυθώ/πλύνω ρούχα;	Pou boro na plitho/plino rouha
Is there somewhere to dry clothes?	Έχει πουθενά μέρος γιά στέγνωμα ρούχων;	Ehi pouthena meros ghia steghnoma rouhon
My butane gas has run out	Μου τέλειωσε το γκάζι	Mou teliosse to gazi
The toilet is blocked	Η τουαλέτα έχει φράξει	I toualeta ehi fraksi

The shower doesn't work/is flooded	Το ντους δεν δουλεύει/ πλημμύρισε	To douz dhen dhoulevi/ plimirisse
What is the voltage?[1]	Πόσα βολτ είναι το ρεύμα;	Possa volt ine to revma
May we light a fire?	Μπορούμε ν'ανάψουμε φωτιά;	Boroume nanapsoume fotia
Please prepare the bill, we are leaving today	Ετοιμάστε σας παρακαλώ το λογαριασμό, φεύγουμε σήμερα	Etimaste sas parakalo to loghariasmo, fevghoume simera
How long do you want to stay?	*Γιά πόσο θα μείνετε;	Ghia posso tha minete
What is your car registration number?	*Ποιός είναι ο αριθμός του αυτοκίνητου σας;	Pios ine o arithmos tou aftokinitou sas
I'm afraid the camp site is full	*Λυπούμε, είμαστε πλήρεις	Lipoume imaste pliris

1. See footnote on p. 59.

YOUTH HOSTELLING

How long is the walk to the youth hostel?	Πόσο απέχει με τα πόδια ο ξενών νεότητος;	Posso apehi me ta podhia o ksenon neotitos
Is there a youth hostel here?	Υπάρχει ξενών νεότητος εδώ;	Iparhi ksenon neotitos edho
Have you a room/bed for the night?	Έχετε δωμάτιο/ κρεβάτι γιά τη νύχτα;	Ehete dhomatio/krevati ghia ti nihta
How many days can we stay?	Πόσες μέρες μπορούμε να μείνουμε;	Posses meres boroume na minoume
Here is my membership card	Να η κάρτα μου μέλους	Na i karta mou melous
Do you serve meals?	Σερβίρετε φαγητό;	Servirete faghito
Can I use the kitchen?	Μπορώ να χρησιμοποιήσω τη κουζίνα;	Boro na hrissimopiisso ti kouzina

Is there somewhere cheap to eat nearby?

Υπάρχει κανένα φθηνό μέρος γιά φαγητό εδώ κοντά;

Iparhi kanena fthino meros ghia faghito edho konda

I want to rent a sheet for my sleeping bag

Θέλω να νοικιάσω ένα σεντόνι γιά τον σάκκο ύπνου μου

Thelo na nikiasso ena sendoni ghia ton sakko ipnou mou

RENTING A PLACE

We have rented an apartment/a villa	Έχουμε νοικιάσει διαμέρισμα/βίλλα	Ehoume nikiassi dhiamerisma/villa
Here is our reservation	Να οι κρατήσεις μας	Na i kratissis mas
Please show us around	Μας δείχνετε τριγύρω	Mas dhihnete trighiro
Does this include the cost of	Συμπεριλαμβάνεται	Simberilamvanete
electricity?	το ηλεκτρικό;	to ilektriko
the gas cylinder?	το γκάζι;	to gazi
the maid?	η υπηρεσία;	i ipiressia
Where is	Που είναι	Pou ine
the electricity mains switch?	ο κεντρικός διακόπτης του ηλεκτρικού;	o kentrikos dhiakoptis tou ilektrikou
the water mains stopcock?	η στρόφιγξ του νερού;	i strofinks tou nerou
the light switch?	ο διακόπτης γιά το φως;	o dhiakoptis ghia to fos
the fuse box?	οι ασφάλειες;	i asfalies

How does the heating/hot water work?	Πως δουλεύει η θέρμανση/το ζεστό νερό;	Pos dhoulevi i thermanssi/to zesto nero
Is there a spare gas cylinder?	Υπάρχει ρεζέρβα του κυλίνδρου γκαζιού;	Iparhi rezerva tou kilindhrou gaziou
Do gas cylinders get delivered?	Φέρνουν στο σπίτι κυλίνδρους γκαζιού;	Fernoun sto spiti kilindhrous gaziou
Please show me how this works	Παρακαλώ δείξτε μου πως λειτουργεί αυτό	Parakalo dhikste mou pos litourghi afto
Which days does the maid come?	Ποιές μέρες έρχεται η υπηρεσία;	Pies meres erhete i ipiressia
For how long?	Γιά πόση ώρα;	Ghia possi ora
Is there a fly screen?	Έχει σίρμα στα παράθυρα;	Ehi sirma sta parathira
When is rubbish collected?	Πότε μαζεύουν τα σκουπίδια;	Pote mazevoun ta skoupidhia
Where can we buy logs for the fire?	Που μπορούμε ν'αγοράσουμε ξύλα γιά το τζάκι;	Pou boroume naghorassoume ksila ghia to dzaki
Is there a barbecue?	Έχει ψησταριά;	Ehi psistaria
Please give me another set of keys	Σας παρακαλώ δώστε μου άλλο ένα ζευγάρι κλειδιά	Sas parakalo dhoste mou alo ena zevghari klidhia
We have replaced the broken ...	Αντικαταστήσαμε τα σπασμένα ...	Andikatastissame ta spasmena
Here is the bill	Να ο λογαριασμός	Na o loghariasmos

| Please return my deposit against breakages | Σας παρακαλώ επιστρέψτε μου την προκαταβολή γιά ζημιές | Sas parakalo epistrepste mou tin prokatavoli ghia zimies |

PROBLEMS

The drain/the pipe/the sink is blocked	Έχει βουλώσει η αποχέτευση/ο σωλήνας/ο νεροχύτης	Ehi voulossi i apohetefsi/o solinas/o nerohitis
The toilet doesn't flush	Δεν τρέχει το νερό στο αποχωρητήριο	Dhen trehi to nero sto apohoritirio
There's no water	Δεν έχει νερό	Dhen ehi nero
We can't turn the water off	Δεν μπορούμε να κλείσουμε το νερό	Dhen boroume na klissoume to nero
We can't turn the shower/tap on	Δεν μπορούμε να ανοίξουμε το ντουζ/τη βρύση	Dhen boroume na aniksoume to douz/ti vrissi
There is a leak	Στάζει νερό	Stazi nero
There is a broken window	Είναι σπασμένο ένα τζάμι	Ine spasmeno ena dzami
The shutters won't close	Δεν κλείνουν τα παντζούρια	Dhen klinoun ta pandzouria
The window won't open	Δεν ανοίγει το παράθυρο	Dhen anighi to parathiro
The electricity has gone off	Δεν έχει ρεύμα	Dhen ehi revma

The heating doesn't work	Δεν δουλεύει η θέρμανση	Dhen dhoulevi i thermanssi
the cooker	η κουζίνα	i kouzina
the refrigerator	το ψυγείο	to psighio
the water heater	ο θερμοσύφωνας	o thermossifonas
The lock is stuck	Μάγκωσε η κλειδαριά	Mangosse i klidharia
This is broken	Αυτό είναι σπασμένο	Afto ine spasmeno
This needs repairing	Αυτό χρειάζεται διόρθωμα	Afto hriazete dhiorthoma
The apartment/villa has been burgled	Έγινε κλοπή στο διαμέρισμα/στη βίλλα	Eghine klopi sto dhiamerisma/sti villa

PARTS OF THE HOUSE

balcony	μπαλκόνι	balconi
bathroom	μπάνιο	banio
bedroom	κρεββατοκάμαρα	krevatokamara
ceiling	ταβάνι	tavani
chimney	καμινάδα	kaminadha
corridor	διάδρομος	dhiadhromos
door	πόρτα	porta
fence	τοίχος	tihos
fireplace	τζάκι	dzaki
floor	πάτωμα	patoma
garage	γκαράζ	garaz
gate	πόρτα	porta

hall	χώλ	hall
kitchen	κουζίνα	kouzina
living room	σαλόνι	saloni
patio	εσωτερική αυλή	essoteriki avli
roof	στέγη	steghi
shutters	παντζούρια	pandzouria
stairs	σκάλες	skales
terrace	ταράτσα	taratsa
wall	τοίχος	tihos
window	παράθυρο	parathiro

FURNITURE AND FITTINGS

armchair	πολυθρόνα	polithrona
barbecue	ψησταριά	psistaria
bath	μπάνιο	banio
bed	κρεββάτι	krevati
blanket	κουβέρτα	kouverta
bolt (*for door*)	σύρτης	sirtis
broom	σκούπα	skoupa
brush	βούρτσα	vourtsa
bucket	κουβάς	kouvas
carpet	χαλί	hali
cassette player	κασσετόφωνο	kassetofono
chair	καρέκλα	karekla
clock	ρολόι	roloi

cooker	κουζίνα μαγειρέματος	kouzina maghirematos
cupboard	ντουλάπι	doulapi
curtains	κουρτίνες	kourtines
cushions	μαξιλάρια	maksilaria
deckchair	σεζλογκ	chaiz long
door	πόρτα	porta
doorbell	κουδούνι	koudhouni
doorknob	χερούλι	herouli
dustbin	κουβάς σκουπιδιών	kouvas skoupidhion
dustpan	φαράσι	farassi
hinge	μεντεσές	mendesses
immersion heater	ηλεκτρικός θερμοσίφωνας	ilektrikos thermossifonas
iron	σίδερο	sidhero
lamp	λάμπα	lamba
lampshade	αμπαξούρ	abazour
light bulb	λάμπα ηλεκτρικού	lamba ilektrikou
lock	κλειδαριά	klidharia
mattress	στρώμα	stroma
mirror	καθρέπτης	kathreptis
mop	σφουγκαρόπανο	sfougaropano
padlock	λουκέτο	louketo
pillow	μαξιλλάρι	maksilari
pipe	σωλήνας	solinas
plug (bath)	βούλωμα μπανιέρας	vouloma banieras

plug (*electric*)	πρίζα	priza
radio	ραδιόφωνο	radhiofono
refrigerator	ψυγείο	psighio
sheet	σεντόνι	sentoni
shelf	ράφι	rafi
shower	ντους	douz
sink	νεροχύτης	nerohitis
sofa	καναπές	kanapes
stool	σκαμνί	skamni
sun-lounger	σεζλογκ	chaiz long
table	τραπέζι	trapezi
tap	βρύση	vrissi
television	τηλεόραση	tileorassi
toilet	τουαλέτα	toualeta
towel	πετσέτα	petseta
vacuum cleaner	ηλεκτρική σκούπα	ilektriki skoupa
washbasin	νυπτήρας	niptiras
washing machine	ηλεκτρικό πλυντήριο	ilektriko plintirio
window catch	γάντσος παραθύρου	ghandzos parathirou
window sill	πρεβάζι	prevazi

KITCHEN EQUIPMENT

| bleach | χλωρίνη | hlorini |
| bottle-opener | ανοιχτήρι γιά μποτίλιες | anihtiri ghia botilies |

bowl	**γαβάθα**	ghavatha
can-opener	**ανοιχτήρι κονσερβών**	anihtiri konservon
candles	**κεριά**	keria
clothes-line	**σχοινί γιά άπλωμα ρούχων**	skhini ghia aploma rouhon
clothes-pegs	**μανταλάκια**	mandalakia
chopping board	**ξύλο όπου κόβουν λαχανικά**	ksilo opou kovoun lahanika
coffee pot	**καφετιέρα**	kafetiera
colander	**τρυπητή**	tripiti
cool-box	**συσκευή ψύξεως**	siskevi psikseos
corkscrew	**τιρμπουσόν**	tirbouson
cup	**φλιντζάνι**	flidzani
detergent	**απορρυπαντικό**	aporipantiko
fork	**πηρούνι**	pirouni
frying pan	**τηγάνι**	tighani
glass	**ποτήρι**	potiri
ice tray	**δίσκος γιά παγάκια**	dhiskos ghia paghakia
kettle	**βραστήρας**	vrastiras
knife	**μαχαίρι**	maheri
matches	**σπίρτα**	spirta
pan	**κατσαρόλα**	katsarola
plate	**πιάτο**	piato
scissors	**ψαλίδι**	psalidhi
sieve (*for flour*)	**κόσκινο**	koskino
spoon	**κουτάλι**	koutali
teatowel	**πετσέτα γιά πιάτα**	petseta ghia piata

torch	φακός	fakos
washing powder	σκόνη σαπούνι	skoni sapouni
washing-up liquid	υγρό γιά πιάτα	ighro ghia piata

ODD JOBS

builder	κτίστης	ktistis
carpenter	μαραγκός	marangos
electrician	ηλεκτρολόγος	ilektrologhos
gardener	κηπουρός	kipouros
painter/decorator	μπογιατζής	boghiadzis
plasterer	σοβατζής	sovadzis
plumber	υδραυλικός	idhravlikos
bracket	υποστήριγμα γιά ράφια	ipostirighma ghia rafia
hammer	σφυρί	sfiri
iron	σίδερο	sidhero
lacquer	λάκκα	laka
metal	μέταλλο	metalo
nails	καρφιά	karfia
paint	μπογιά	boghia
paint brush	πινέλο γιά βάψιμο	pinelo ghia vapsimo
plastic	πλαστικό	plastiko
pliers	τανάλια	tanalia
saw	πριόνι	prioni
screwdriver	κατσαβίδι	katsavidhi

screws	βίδες	vidhes
spanner	κλειδί	klidhi
steel	ατσάλι	atsali
tile/roof tile	πλακάκι/κεραμίδι	plakaki/keramidhi
wire/electrical wire	σύρμα/καλώδιο	sirma/kalodhio
wood	ξύλο	ksilo

MEETING PEOPLE

How are you?	**Πως είσαι/πως τα πας;**	Pos isse/pos ta pas
How are things?	**Πως είναι τα πράγματα;**	Pos ine ta praghmata
Fine, thanks, and you?	**Καλά ευχαριστώ, κι εσύ;**	Kala efharisto, ki essi
My name is ...	**Το όνομα μου είναι ...**	To onoma mou ine
May I introduce ...	**Να σας συστήσω ...**	Na sas sistisso
This is ...	**Αυτός** (*masc.*)/**Αυτή** (*fem.*) **είναι ...**	Aftos/afti ine
Have you met ...?	**Έχετε συναντήσει τον** (*masc.*)/**την** (*fem.*) **...;**	Ehete sinantissi ton/tin
Glad to meet you	**Χαίρω πολύ**	Hero poli
Am I disturbing you?	**Σας ενοχλώ;**	Sas enohlo
Sorry to have troubled you	**Συγγνώμη για την ενόχληση**	Sighnomi ghia tin enohlissi

What lovely/awful weather	**Τι ωραίος/απαίσιος καιρός**	Ti oreos/apessios keros
It is cold/hot today	**Κάνει κρύο/ζέστη σήμερα**	Kani krio/zesti simera
Do you think it's going to rain/snow?	**Νομίζετε ότι θα βρέξει/θα χιονίσει;**	Nomizete oti tha vreksi/ tha hionissi
Will it be sunny tomorrow?	**Θα έχει λιακάδα αύριο;**	Tha ehi liakadha avrio
Go away	**Φύγετε**	Fighete
Leave me alone	**Αφήστε με μόνο (*masc.*)/μόνη (*fem.*) μου**	Afiste me mono/moni mou

MAKING FRIENDS

Is this your first visit?	***Είναι η πρώτη φορά που έρχεστε εδώ;**	Ine i proti fora pou erheste edho
Do you like it here?	***Σας αρέσει εδώ;**	Sas aressi edho
Are you staying here?	***Μένετε εδώ;**	Menete edho
We've been here a week	**Είμαστε εδώ μια εβδομάδα**	Imaste edho mia evdhomadha
Are you on your own?	**Είσαστε μόνος (*masc.*)/μόνη (*fem.*) σας;**	Issaste monos/moni sas
I am travelling alone	**Ταξιδεύω μόνος μου (*masc.*)/μόνη μου (*fem.*)**	Taksidhevo monos mou/ moni mou
I am with	**Είμαι με**	Ime me

my husband/my wife	του άνδρα μου/τη γυναίκα μου	ton andhra mou/ti ghineka mou
my parents	τους γονείς μου	tous ghonis mou
my family	την οικογένεια μου	tin ikoghenia mou
a friend	έναν φίλο (*masc.*)/ μια φίλη (*fem.*)	enan filo/mia fili
Are you married/ single?	Είσαστε παντρεμένος (*masc.*)/-η (*fem.*)/ ελεύθερος/-η;	Issaste pandremenos/-i/ eleftheros/-i
Do you have children?	Έχετε παιδιά;	Ehete pedhia
Do you travel a lot?	Ταξιδεύετε συχνά;	Taksidhevete sihna
Do you mind if I smoke?	Σας πειράζει να καπνίσω;	Sas pirazi na kapnisso
Help yourself	Πάρτε μόνος (*masc.*)/μόνη (*fem.*) σας	Parte monos/moni sas
Where do you come from?	Από που είσαστε;	Apo pou issaste
I come from ...	Είμαι από την ...	Ime apo tin
Have you been to England/America?	Έχετε πάει στην Αγγλία/Αμερική;	Ehete pai stin anglia/ ameriki
What do you do?	Τι κάνετε;	Ti kanete
What are you studying?	Τι σπουδάζετε;	Ti spoudhazete
I'm on holiday/ a (*business*) trip	Κάνω τις διακοπές μου/ταξίδι (γιά δουλειά)	Kano tis dhiakopes mou/ taksidhi (ghia dhoulia)
I hope to see you again	Ελπίζω να σας ξαναδώ	Elpizo na sas ksanadho

INVITATIONS

Would you like to have lunch tomorrow?	**Θέλετε να φάμε μαζί αύριο το μεσημέρι;**	Thelete na fame mazi avrio to messimeri
Can you come to dinner/for a drink?	**Μπορείτε να έρθετε να φάμε μαζί/για ένα ποτό;**	Borite na erthete na fame mazi/ghia ena poto
We're giving/there is a party	**Δίνουμε/γίνεται ένα πάρτυ**	Dhinoume/ghinete ena parti
Would you like to come?	**Θέλετε να έρθετε;**	Thelete na erthete
Can I bring a friend?	**Μπορώ να φέρω ένα φίλο** *m.***/μια φίλη** *f.***;**	Boro na fero ena filo *m.*/ mia fili
Thanks for the invitation	**Ευχαριστώ για την πρόσκληση**	Efharisto ghia tin prosklissi
I'd love to come	**Θα ήθελα πολύ να έρθω**	Tha ithela poli na ertho
I'm sorry, I can't come	**Λυπούμαι, αλλά δεν μπορώ να έρθω**	Lipoume, alla dhen boro na ertho
Can I get you a drink?	**Μπορώ να σας προσφέρω ένα ποτό;**	Boro na sas prosfero ena poto
I'd like a ..., please	**Θα ήθελα ένα ... παρακαλώ**	Tha ithela ena ... parakalo
Could we have coffee/a drink somewhere?	**Μπορούμε να πάμε για καφέ/για κανένα ποτό πουθενά;**	Boroume na pame ghia kafe/ghia kanena poto pouthena

Shall we go to the cinema?	Θέλετε να πάμε στο κινηματογράφο;	Thelete na pame sto kinimatoghrafo
theatre?	στο θέατρο;	sto theatro
beach?	στην παραλία;	stin paralia
Would you like to go dancing/for a drive?	Θέλετε να πάμε να χορέψουμε/γιά μιά βόλτα με τ'αυτοκίνητο;	Thelete na pame na horepsoume/ghia mia volta me taftokinito
Do you know a good disco/restaurant?	Ξέρετε καμμιά καλή ντισκοτέκ/ εστιατόριο;	Kserete kamia kali discotheque/estiatorio
Where shall we meet?	Που να συναντηθούμε;	Pou na sinantithoume
What time shall I/we come?	Τι ώρα να έρθω/ έρθουμε;	Ti ora na ertho/erthoume
I could pick you up at ...	Θα μπορούσα να σας συναντήσω στο ...	Tha boroussa na sas sinantisso sto
Could you meet me at ...?	Θα μπορούσατε να με συναντήσετε στις ...	Tha boroussate na me sinantissete stis
Can we give you a lift home/to your hotel?	Μπορούμε να σας πάμε στον σπίτι/ στο ξενοδοχείο σας;	Boroume na sas pame ston spiti/sto ksenodhohio sas
Can I see you again?	Μπορώ να σας ξαναδώ;	Boro na sas ksanadho
Where do you live?	Που μένετε;	Pou menete
What is your telephone number?	Ποιός είναι ο αριθμός του τηλεφώνου σας;	Pios ine o arithmos tou tilefonou sas

Thanks for the evening/drink/ride	Σας ευχαριστώ για το βράδυ/το ποτό/τη βόλτα	Sas efharisto ghia to vradhi/to poto/ti volta
It was lovely	Ήταν πολύ ωραία	Itan poli orea
Hope to see you again soon	Ελπίζω να σας ξαναδώ σύντομα	Elpizo na sas ksanadho sintoma
See you soon/later/tomorrow	Θα σας δω σύντομα/αργότερα/αύριο	Tha sas dho sintoma/arghotera/avrio

GOING TO A RESTAURANT

Can you suggest a good cheap restaurant?	Μπορείτε να μου συστήσετε ένα καλό φθηνό εστιατόριο;	Borite na mou sistissete ena kalo fthino estiatorio
I'd like to book a table for four at 1 p.m.	Θέλω να κλείσω ένα τραπέζι γιά τέσσερεις στις μία η ώρα	Thelo na klisso ena trapezi ghia tesseris stis mia i ora
I've reserved a table. My name is ...	Έχω κλείσει τραπέζι. Λέγομαι ...	Eho klissi trapezi. Leghome
We did not make a reservation	Δεν έχουμε κλείσει τραπέζι	Dhen ehoume klissi trapezi
Have you a table for three?	Έχετε ένα τραπέζι γιά τρεις;	Ehete ena trapezi ghia tris
You would have to wait about ... minutes	*Θα πρέπει να περιμένετε περίπου ... λεπτά	Tha prepi na perimenete peripou ... lepta

Is there a table	Έχετε κανένα τραπέζι	Ehete kanena trapezi
on the terrace?	στην ταράτσα;	stin taratsa
by the window?	κοντά στο παράθυρο;	konta sto parathiro
in a corner?	στην γωνία;	stin ghonia
We shall have a table free in half an hour	*Θα έχουμε ένα τραπέζι σε μισή ώρα	Tha ehoume ena trapezi se missi ora
Is there a non-smoking area?	Υπάρχει χώρος γιά τους μη καπνίζοντες;	Iparhi horos ghia tous mi kapnizontes
We don't serve lunch until 12.30	*Δεν σερβίρουμε μεσημεριανό πριν απ'τίς δωδεκάμιση	Dhen serviroume messimeriano prin aptis dhodhekamissi
We don't serve dinner until 8 o'clock	*Δεν σερβίρουμε βραδυνό πρίν απ'τίς οκτώ	Dhen serviroume vradhino prin aptis okto
We stop serving at 11 o'clock	*Δεν σερβίρουμε μετά απ'τίς έντεκα	Dhen serviroume meta aptis endeka
Sorry, the kitchen is closed	*Συγγνώμη, η κουζίνα έκλεισε	Sighnomi, i kouzina eklisse
Where is the cloakroom?	Που είναι η γκαρνταρόμπα;	Pou ine i gardaroba
It is downstairs	*Είναι κάτω	Ine kato
We are in a hurry	Βιαζόμαστε	Viazomaste
Do you serve snacks?	Έχετε μεζέδες;	Ehete mezedhes
That was an excellent meal	Περίφημο γεύμα	Perifimo ghevma

| We shall come again | **Θα ξανάρθουμε** | Tha ksanarthoume |

ORDERING

Service charge	***Ποσοστά σερβιτόρου**	Possosta servitorou
Service (not) included	**Τα ποσοστά (δεν) συμπεριλαμβάνονται**	Ta possosta (dhen) simperilamvanonte
Cover charge	***Κουβέρ**	Kouver
Waiter/waitress	**Σερβιτόρος/ σερβιτόρα**	Servitoros/servitora
May I see the menu/ the wine list, please?	**Μπορώ να δω το μενού παρακαλώ/ την λίστα κρασιών;**	Boro na dho to menou parakalo/tin lista krassion
Is there a set menu for lunch?	**Είναι το μεσημεριανό φαγητό τάμπλ-ντότ**	Ine to messimeriano faghito table d'hôte
What is your dish of the day?	**Ποιό είναι το πιάτο της μέρας;**	Pio ine to piato tis meras
Do you have any vegetarian dishes?	**Έχετε φαγητά γιά χορτοφάγους;**	Ehete faghita ghia hortofaghous
I want something light	**Θέλω κάτι ελαφρό**	Thelo kati elafro
Do you have children's helpings?	**Έχετε μερίδες γιά παιδιά;**	Ehete meridhes ghia pedhia
What do you recommend?	**Τί μου συστήνετε;**	Ti mou sistinete
What is this?	**Τί είναι αυτό;**	Ti ine afto

What are the specialities of the restaurant/of the region?	**Ποιές είναι οι σπεσιαλιτέ σας/της περιοχής;**	Pies ine i spessialite sas/ tis periohis
Would you like to try ...?	***Θέλετε να δοκιμάσετε ...;***	Thelete na dhokimassete
There's no more ...	***Τέλειωσε το ...***	Teliosse to
I'd like ...	**Θα ήθελα ...**	Tha ithela
Is it hot or cold?	**Είναι ζεστό η κρύο;**	Ine zesto i krio

COMPLAINTS

Where are our drinks?	**Που είναι τα ποτά μας;**	Pou ine ta pota mas
Why is the food taking so long?	**Γιατί αργεί τόσο να έρθη το φαγητό;**	Ghiati arghi tosso na erthi to faghito
This isn't what I ordered. I want ...	**Δεν παράγγειλα αυτό. Θέλω ...**	Dhen parangila afto. Thelo
I don't want any oil/ sauce wiih it	**Δεν θέλω λάδι/ σάλτσα**	Dhen thelo ladhi/saltsa
Some more bread, please	**Λίγο ακόμα ψωμί παρακαλώ**	Ligho akoma psomi parakalo
A little more, please	**Λίγο ακόμα παρακαλώ**	Ligho akoma parakalo

This is	Αυτό είναι	Afto ine
bad	χαλασμένο	halasmeno
uncooked	άψητο	apsito
stale	μπαγιάτικο	baghiatiko
overcooked	πολύ ψημένο	poli psimeno

| This is cold/salty | Αυτό είναι κρύο/ αλμυρό | Afto ine krio/almiro |

| This isn't fresh | Δεν είναι φρέσκο αυτό | Dhen ine fresko afto |

| This plate/knife/ spoon/glass is not clean | Αυτό το πιάτο/ μαχαίρι/κουτάλι/ ποτήρι δεν είναι καθαρό | Afto to piato/maheri/ koutali/potiri dhen ine katharo |

| I'd like to see the head waiter | Θέλω να δω τον αρχι σερβιτόρο | Thelo na dho ton arhi servitoro |

PAYING

| The bill, please | Παρακαλώ το λογαριασμό | Parakalo to loghariasmo |

| Does it include service? | Συμπεριλαμβάνει το σερβίς; | Simberilamvani to servis |

| Please check the bill – I don't think it's correct | Ξανακάντε το λογαριασμό σας παρακαλώ – νομίζω ότι είναι λάθος | Ksanakante to loghariasmo sas parakalo – nomizo oti ine lathos |

| What is this amount for? | Τί αντιπροσωπεύει αυτό το ποσό; | Ti antiprossopevi afto to posso |

| I didn't have soup | Δεν πήρα σούπα | Dhen pira soupa |

I had chicken, not steak	Πήρα κοτόπουλο, όχι μπιφτέκι	Pira kotopoulo, ohi bifteki
May we have separate bills?	Μπορούμε να χούμε ξεχωριστούς λογαριασμούς;	Boroume na houme ksehoristous loghariasmous
Do you take credit cards/travellers' cheques?	Παίρνετε κάρτες πιστώσεως/ τράβελλερς τσέκς;	Pernete kartes pistoseos/ travellers' cheques
Keep the change	Κρατήστε τα ρέστα	Kratiste ta resta
It was very nice	Ήταν πολύ ωραία	Itan poli orea
We enjoyed it, thank you	Το ευχαριστηθήκαμε, σας ευχαριστούμε	To efharistithikame, sas efharistoume

BREAKFAST AND TEA

What time is breakfast served?	Τι ώρα σερβίρεται το πρόγευμα;	Ti ora servirete to proghevma
A large white coffee, please	Ένα νεσκαφέ με γάλα παρακαλώ	Ena nescafé me ghala parakalo
A black coffee	Ένα νεσκαφέ χωρίς γάλα	Ena nescafé horis ghala
Greek coffee (bitter, medium, sweet)	Ελληνικό καφέ (χωρίς ζάχαρη, μέτριο, γλυκό)	Elliniko kafe (horis zahari, metrio, ghliko)
I would like a decaffeinated coffee	Θα ήθελα ένα καφέ ντεκαφεϊνέ	Tha ithela ena kafe dekafeïne
A cup of tea, please	Ένα φλιτζάνι τσάι παρακαλώ	Ena flidzani tsai parakalo

I'd like tea with milk/lemon	Θέλω τσάι με γάλα/λεμόνι	Thelo tsai me ghala/lemoni
I would like a camomile	Θα ήθελα ένα χαμομήλι	Tha ithela ena hamomili
May we have some sugar, please?	Λίγη ζάχαρη παρακαλώ;	Lighi zahari parakalo
Do you have saccharine?	Έχετε ζαχαρίνη;	Ehete zaharini
Hot/cold milk	Ζεστό/κρύο γάλα	Zesto/krio ghala
A roll and butter	Ένα ψωμάκι και βούτυρο	Ena psomaki ke voutiro
Toast/rusk	Φρυγανιά	Frighania
Bread	Ψωμί	Psomi
We'd like more butter, please	Λίγο ακόμα βούτυρο παρακαλώ	Ligho akoma voutiro parakalo
Have you some jam/honey?	Έχετε λίγη μαρμελάδα/μέλι;	Ehete lighi marmeladha/meli
I'd like	Θέλω	Thelo
a soft-boiled egg	ένα βραστό νερουλό αυγό	ena vrasto neroulo avgho
a hard-boiled egg	ένα σφιχτό αυγό	ena sfihto avgho
fried eggs	τηγανητά αυγά	tighanita avgha
What fruit juices do you have?	Τί χυμούς φρούτων έχετε;	Ti himous frouton ehete
Orange/grapefruit/tomato juice	Πορτοκάλι/γκρέιπφρούτ/ντοματόζουμο	Portokali/grapefruit/domatozoumo
Fresh fruit	Φρέσκα φρούτα	Freska frouta
(Drinking) chocolate	Κακάο	Kakao
Yoghurt	Γιαούρτι	Ghiaourti

Pastry[1]	Πάστες	Pastes
Cake	Κέϊκ	Cake
Help yourself at the buffet	*Σερβιριστείτε μόνοι σας στο μπουφές	Serviristite moni sas sto boufes

SNACKS AND PICNICS

Can I have a ... sandwich, please?	Μπορώ να έχω ένα σάντουιτς με ... παρακαλώ;	Boro na eho ena sandovits me ... parakalo
What are those things over there?	Τί είναι αυτά εκεί;	Ti ine afta eki
What are they made of?	Με τί είναι καμωμένα;	Me ti ine kamomena
What is in them?	Τί περιέχουν;	Ti periehoun
I'll have one of these, please	Θα πάρω ένα απ'αυτά παρακαλώ	Tha paro ena apafta parakalo
biscuits	μπισκότα	biscota
roll	φραντζολάκι	frandzolaki
bread	ψωμί	psomi
butter	βούτυρο	voutiro
cheese	τυρί	tiri
chips	πατατάκια	patatakia
chocolate bar	σοκολάτα	sokolata
egg(s)	αυγό (-ά)	avgho (-a)

1. For names of cakes and pastry, see p. 107.

ham	**ζαμπόν**	zambon
ice cream (*flavours: page 108*)	**παγωτό**	paghoto
pickles	**τουρσί**	toursi
meat/fruit pie	**κρεατόπιττα/ φρουτόπιττα**	kreatopita/froutopita
salad	**σαλάτα**	salata
sausage	**λουκάνικο**	loukaniko
snack	**μεζές**	mezes
soup	**σούπα**	soupa
tomato	**ντομάτα**	domata

DRINKS[1]

Bar/café	**Μπάρ**	Bar
Coffee house	**Καφενείο**	Kafenio
What will you have to drink?	***Τί θα πιείτε;**	Ti tha piite
A bottle of the local wine, please	**Ένα μπουκάλι ντόπιο κρασί παρακαλώ**	Ena boukali dopio krassi parakalo
Do you serve wine by the glass?	**Σερβίρετε κρασί με το ποτήρι;**	Servirete krassi me to potiri
Carafe/glass	**Καράφα/ποτήρι**	Karafa/potiri
Bottle/half bottle	**Μποτίλια/μισή μποτίλια**	Botilia/missi botilia

1. For the names of beverages, see p. 110.

Two glasses of beer, please	Δύο ποτήρια μπύρα παρακαλώ	Dhio potiria bira parakalo
Large/small beer	Μεγάλη/μικρή μπύρα	Meghali/mikri bira
Two more beers	Δύο ακόμα μπύρες	Dhio akoma bires
Neat/straight up	Σκέτο/ως επάνω	Sketo/os epano
On the rocks	Μόνο με πάγο	Mono me pagho
Ice cubes	Παγάκια	Paghakia
With soda/water	Με σόδα/νερό	Me sodha/nero
Mineral water	Μεταλλικό νερό	Metaliko nero
Soft drinks	Αναψυκτικά	Anapsiktika
Do you serve cocktails?	Έχετε κοκτέιλς;	Ehete cocktails
I'd like	Θέλω	Thelo
a long soft drink with ice	ένα μεγάλο αναψυκτικό με πάγο	ena meghalo anapsiktiko me pagho
an apple juice	χυμός μήλου	himos milou
an orange juice	πορτοκαλάδα	portokaladha
a fruit juice	χυμός φρούτων	himos frouton
an iced coffee	φραπέ	frape
an iced tea	παγωμένο τσάι	paghomeno tsai
beer	μπύρα	bira
dark	μαύρη	mavri
light	ελαφριά	elafria
bottled	σε μπουκάλι	se boukali
in a can	σε κονσέρβα	se konserva
draught	χύμα	hima
hot chocolate	ζεστή σοκολάτα	zesti sokolata
tea	τσάι	tsai
herb	του βουνού	tou vounou

camomile	του χαμομήλι	tou hamomili
mint	του μέντα	tou menda
lime	του τύλιο	tou tilio
grape juice	χυμός σταφυλιών	himos stafilion
grapefruit juice	γκρέιπφρουτζουμο	grapefruit-zoumo
tomato juice	ντοματόζουμο	domatozoumo
on the rocks	με πάγο μόνο	me pagho mono
I'd like another glass of water, please	Άλλο ένα ποτήρι νερό παρακαλώ	Alo ena potiri nero parakalo
The same again, please	Ξανά το ίδιο παρακαλώ	Ksana to idhio parakalo
Three black coffees and one with milk	Τρεις νεσκαφέ χωρίς γάλα κιένα με γάλα	Tris nescafé horis ghala kiena me ghala
Greek coffee (bitter, medium, sweet)	Ελληνικό καφέ (χωρίς ζάχαρη, μέτριο, γλυκό)	Elliniko kafe (horis zahari, metrio, ghliko)
May we have an ashtray?	Ένα τασάκι παρακαλώ;	Ena tasaki parakalo
Can I have a light, please?	Έχετε φωτιά παρακαλώ;	Ehete fotia parakalo

RESTAURANT VOCABULARY

artificial sweetener/ saccharine	ζαχαρίνη	zaharini
ashtray	τασάκι	tasaki
bill	λογαριασμός	loghariasmos
bowl	γαβάδα	ghavatha

bread	ψωμί	psomi
butter	βούτυρο	voutiro
cigarettes	τσιγάρα	tsighara
cloakroom	γκαρνταρόμπα	gardaroba
course (*dish*)	πιάτο	piato
cream	κρέμα	krema
cup	φλιτζάνι	flidzani
fork	πηρούνι	pirouni
glass	ποτήρι	potiri
hungry (to be)	πεινάω	pinao
knife	μαχαίρι	maheri
matches	σπίρτα	spirta
menu	μενού κατάλογος	menou kataloghos
mustard	μουστάρδα	moustardha
napkin	πετσέτα	petseta
oil	λάδι	ladhi
pepper	πιπέρι	piperi
plate	πιάτο	piato
restaurant	εστιατόριο	estiatorio
salt	αλάτι	alati
sauce	σάλτσα	saltsa
saucer	πιατάκι	piataki
service	υπηρεσία	ipiressia
spoon	κουτάλι	koutali
sugar	ζάχαρη	zahari
table	τραπέζι	trapezi

tablecloth	τραπεζομάντηλο	trapezomandilo
terrace	ταράτσα	taratsa
thirsty (to be)	διψώ	dhipso
tip	πουρμπουάρ	pourbouar
toothpick	οδοντογλυφίδα	odhontoghlifidha
vegetarian	χορτοφάγος	hortofaghos
vinegar	ξύδι	xidhi
waiter	σερβιτόρος	servitoros
waitress	σερβιτόρα	servitora
water	νερό	nero

THE MENU

ΣΟΥΠΕΣ	soupes	SOUPS
αυγολέμονο	avgholemono	egg and lemon soup
κονσομέ	consommé	consommé
κοτόσουπα	kotossoupa	chicken soup
ντοματόσουπα	domatossoupa	tomato soup
σούπα λαχανικών	soupa lahanikon	vegetable soup
σούπα φακιές	soupa fakies	lentil soup
σούπα φασόλια	soupa fassolia	bean soup
τραχανάς	trahanas	pasta soup
φιδές	fidhes	vermicelli soup
ψαρόσουπα	psarossoupa	fish soup

ΜΕΖΕΔΕΣ	mezede	HORS D'OEUVRES
αγκινάρες αλά πολίτα	anginares ala polita	artichokes cooked in olive oil, with onions and potatoes
αυγοτάραχο	avghotaraho	dry cod roe
γεμιστές μελιτζάνες	ghemistes melidzanes	stuffed aubergines
γεμιστές ντομάτες	ghemistes domates	stuffed tomatoes
γεμιστές πιπεριές	ghemistes piperies	stuffed peppers
ελιές	elies	olives
θαλασσινά	thalassina	shellfish, sea food
καλαμαράκια	kalamarakia	fried baby squid
μαρίδες	maridhes	whitebait
μελιτζανοσαλάτα	melidzanosalata	aubergine salad
μπρίκ	brik	red caviar
ντολμάδες, ντολμαδάκια	dolmadhes, dolmadhakia	stuffed cabbage, vine leaves
σαχανάκι	sahanaki	fried cheese
σκορδαλιά	skordhalia	garlic dip
ταραμάς	taramas	cod roe
ταραμοσαλάτα	taramosalata	cod roe salad
τζατζίκι	tzatziki	cucumber and yogurt salad
φασολάκια πλακί	fassolakia plaki	dried beans cooked in olive oil and tomatoes
(μάυρο) χαβιάρι	(mavro) haviari	(black) caviar

ZYMAPIKA	zimarika	PASTA
κριθαράκι	kritharaki	rice-shaped pasta
μακαρόνια	makaronia	spaghetti
παστίτσιο	pastitsio	baked macaroni
χυλοπίτες	hilopites	short noodles

PIZI	rizi	RICE
πιλάφι	pilafi	rice pilaf
πιλάφι με γιαούρτι	pilafi me ghiaourti	rice with yoghurt
πιλάφι με μύδια	pilafi me midhia	rice with mussels
πιλάφι με μπιζελάκια	pilafi me bizelakia	rice with peas
πιλάφι με συκωτάκια	pilafi me sikotakia	rice with liver
σπανακόριζο	spanakorizo	rice with spinach

ΨΑΡΙΑ	psaria	FISH
άστακός	astakos	lobster
αχινοί	ahini	sea urchins
γαρίδες	gharides	shrimp
γλώσσα	ghlossa	sole
ξιφίος	ksifios	swordfish

καβούρι	kavouri	crab
καλαμάρια	kalamaria	squid
κέφαλος	kefalos	mullet
λυθρίνι	lithrini	bream
μαρίδες	maridhes	whitebait
μπακαλιάρος	bakaliaros	dry salted cod
μπαρμπούνι	barbouni	red mullet
οκταπόδι	oktapodhi	octopus
σαρδέλες	sardheles	sardines
σκουμπρί	skoubri	mackerel
σολομός	solomos	salmon
σουπιές	soupies	ink fish
συναγρίδα	sinaghridha	red snapper
τηγανιτά ψάρια	tighanita psaria	fried fish
τόννος	tonos	tunny/tuna
τσιπούρα	tsipoura	gilthead bream
ψάρι σχάρας	psari skharas	grilled fish
ψητό ψάρι	psito psari	baked fish

ΚΡΕΑΣ	kreas	MEAT
αρνάκι σούβλας	arnaki souvlas	lamb on the spit
αρνί	arni	lamb
αρνίσιες μπριζόλες	arnissies brizoles	lamb chops
(βραστό) βοδινό	(vrasto) vodhino	(boiled) beef

γλώσσα	ghlossa	tongue
κεφτέδες	keftedhes	meat balls
κοκορέτσι	kokoretsi	lamb innards on the spit (intestines, liver, spleen, kidneys, heart)
λουκάνικα	loukanika	sausages
μοσχαρίσιες μπριζόλες	moskharissies brizoles	veal chops
μουσακάς	moussakas	moussaka
μπιφτέκι	bifteki	steak
μπριζόλα	brizola	chop
μυαλά	miala	brains
νεφρά	nefra	kidneys
παϊδάκια	paeedhakia	lamb cutlets
σουβλάκια	souvlakia	kebab
συκώτι	sikoti	liver
(σχάρας) φιλέτο	(skharas) (fileto)	(grilled) steak
χοιρινές μπριζόλες	hirines brizoles	pork chops
ψητό	psito	roast
(ψητό) μοσχαράκι	(psito) moskharaki	(roast) veal
ψητό χοιρινού	psito hirinou	roast pork

ΠΟΥΛΕΡΙΚΑ	poulerika	POULTRY
γαλοπούλα	ghalopoula	turkey
κοτόπουλο	kotopoulo	chicken
πάπια	papia	duck
πόδι κότας	podhi kotas	leg of chicken
στήθος κότας	stithos kotas	chicken breast
φασιανός	fassianos	pheasant
χήνα	hina	goose
ψητό κοτόπουλο στη σούβλα	psito kotopoulo sti souvla	spit roasted chicken

ΛΑΧΑΝΙΚΑ ΚΑΙ ΣΑΛΑΤΕΣ	lahanika ke salates	VEGETABLES AND SALAD
αγγούρι	angouri	cucumber
αγκινάρες	anginares	artichokes
γίγαντες	ghighantes	broad beans
καλαμπόκι	kalamboki	corn
καρότα	karota	carrots
κολοκυθάκια	kolokithakia	courgettes
κουκκιά	koukia	fava beans
κουνουπίδι	kounoupidhi	cauliflower
κρεμμύδι	kremidhi	onion
λάχανο	lahano	cabbage
μαϊντανός	maïdanos	parsley

μανιτάρια	manitaria	mushrooms
μαρούλι	marouli	lettuce
μελιτζάνες	melidzanes	aubergine
μπάμιες	bamies	okra
μπιζέλια	bizelia	peas
ντομάτες	domates	tomatoes
παντζάρια	pandzaria	beetroot
πατάτες	patates	potatoes
πιπεριές	piperies	peppers
πράσα	prassa	leeks
ραδίκια	radhikia	dandelions
ραπανάκια	rapanakia	radishes
ρεβίθια	revithia	chick-peas
σέλινο	selino	celery
σκόρδο	skordho	garlic
σπανάκι	spanaki	spinach
σπαράγγια	sparangia	asparagus
φακιές	fakies	lentils
φρέσκα φασολάκια	freska fassolakia	green beans

ΑΥΓΑ	avgha	**EGGS**
αυγά (τηγανιτά)μάτια	avgha (tighanita)matia	(fried) eggs
βραστά αυγά	vrasta avgha	boiled eggs
ομελέτα	omeleta	omelette

ΤΥΡΙΑ	tyria	CHEESES
κασέρι	kasseri	(the nearest to Cheddar, but made of sheep's milk, and smoother and richer)
κεφαλοτύρι	kefalotiri	(very salty version of kasseri, almost like Parmesan)
μανούρι	manouri	(white, almost no salt added, very creamy)
ροκφόρ	rokfor	blue cheese
φέτα	feta	(white, sharp and salty, often made of sheep's or goat's milk)

ΓΛΥΚΙΣΜΑΤΑ	ghlikismata	DESSERTS
γαλακτομπούρεκο	ghalaktoboureko	very thin crispy pastry with custard and syrup
γιαούρτι	ghiaourti	yoghurt
καταίφι	kataifi	finely shredded pastry with nuts and syrup or honey
κέϊκ	cake	cake/gâteau
κομπόστα	komposta	stewed fruit

κρέμα	krema	cream
κρεμ καραμέλ	crem karamel	crème caramel
λουκούμι	loukoumi	Turkish delight
μπακλαβάς	baklavas	very thin crispy pastry with nuts and syrup or honey
παγωτό	paghoto	ice cream
βανίλια	vanilia	vanilla
βύσσινο	vissino	cherry
κασάτα	kassata	cassata
λεμόνι	lemoni	lemon
σοκολάτα	sokolata	chocolate
πάστες	pastes	pastry
τούρτα	tourta	trifle
φρουτοσαλάτα	froutosalata	fruit salad

ΦΡΟΥΤΑ ΚΑΙ ΞΗΡΟΙ ΚΑΡΠΟΙ	frouta ke ksiri karpi	**FRUIT AND NUTS**

βερίκοκκα	verikoka	apricots
ροδάκινα	rodhakina	peaches
πορτοκάλι	portokali	orange
σταφύλια	stafilia	grapes
πεπόνι	peponi	melon
καρπούζι	karpouzi	water melon
λεμόνι	lemoni	lemon
κυδώνι	kidhoni	quince

μπανάνα	banana	banana
κεράσια	kerassia	cherries
μούσμουλα	mousmoula	loquats
σύκα	sika	figs
δαμάσκηνα	dhamaskina	prunes
φράουλες	fraoules	strawberries
μούρα	moura	mulberries
αμύγδαλα	amighdhala	almonds
καρύδια	karidhia	walnuts
σταφίδες	stafidhes	raisins
μήλο	milo	apple
αχλάδι	ahladhi	pear
φυστίκια	fistikia	pistachios

ΤΡΟΠΟΙ ΜΑΓΕΙΡΕΜΑΤΟΣ	tropi maghirematos	WAYS OF COOKING
βραστό	vrasto	boiled/stewed
γεμιστό	ghemisto	stuffed
ζεστό/κρύο	zesto/krio	hot/cold
καπνιστό	kapnisto	smoked
κοκκινιστό	kokinisto	cooked with butter and tomatoes

κρέας	kreas	meat
άψητο	apsito	underdone
καλοψημένο	kalopsimeno	well done
μέτρια ψημένο	metria psimeno	medium
σενιάν	senian	rare
μαρινάτο	marinato	marinated
με βούτυρο/λάδι	me voutiro/ladhi	with butter/oil
με μαϊντανό	me maidano	with parsley
ποσσαρισμένο	possarismeno	poached
πουρέ	purée	puréed/creamed
στον αχνό	ston ahno	steamed
στη σχάρα	sti skhara	grilled
τηγανιτό	tighanito	fried
της κατσαρόλας	tis katsarolas	braised
τριμμένο	trimeno	grated
ψητό	psito	baked/roast
ψητό στα κάρβουνα	psito sta karvouna	barbecued
ωμό	omo	raw

ΠΟΤΑ	pota	DRINKS
γάλα	ghala	milk
γκαζόζα	gazoza	lemonade
Ελληνικό καφές (χωρίς ζάχαρη, μέτριος, γλυκός)	elliniko kafes (horis zahari, metrios, ghlikos)	Greek coffee (without sugar, medium, sweet)
καφές/νεσκαφέ	kafes/nescafé	coffee

WAYS OF COOKING · 111

κονιάκ	koniak	cognac
κρασί	krassi	wine
ξερό/γλυκό	ksero/ghliko	dry/sweet
κόκκινο	kokino	red
άσπρο	aspro	white
ροζέ/κοκκινέλι	rosé/kokineli	rosé
παγωμένο	paghomeno	chilled
σε θερμοκρασία	se thermokrassia	at room temperature
δωματίου	dhomatiou	
λεμονάδα	lemonadha	lemonade (made with lemon juice)
μεταλλικό νερό	metaliko nero	mineral water
μπύρα	bira	beer
νερό	nero	water
πορτοκαλάδα	portokaladha	orangeade
ρετσίνα	retsina	resinated white wine
χυμός φρούτων	himos frouton	fruit juice

SHOPPING[1] & SERVICES

Which is the best …?	Ποιός (-ά, -ό) είναι ο (η, το) καλύτερος (-η, -ο) …;	Pios (pia, pio) ine o (i, to) kaliteros (-i, -o)
Where is the nearest …?	Που είναι το πλησιέστερο …;	Pou ine to plissiestero
Where are the best department stores?	Που είναι τα καλύτερα μαγαζιά;	Pou ine ta kalitera maghazia
Where is the market?	Που είναι η αγορά;	Pou ine i aghora
Is there a market every day?	Είναι ανοιχτή η αγορά κάθε μέρα;	Ine anikti i aghora kathe mera

1. Shopping hours are 8.30 a.m. to 1.45 p.m. and 5 p.m. to 10 p.m. from May to October, and 8.30 a.m. to 1.15 p.m. and 4 p.m. to 7.30 p.m. the rest of the year.

Where's the nearest chemist?	Που είναι το πλησιέστερο φαρμακείο;	Pou ine to plissiestero farmakio
Where can I buy ...?	Που μπορώ ν'αγοράσω ...;	Pou boro n'aghorasso
When do the shops open/close?	Πότε ανοίγουν/ κλείνουν τα μαγαζιά;	Pote anighoun/klinoun ta maghazia
Can you recommend a ...?	Μπορείτε να μου συστήσετε ένα ...;	Borite na mou sistissete ena

SHOPS AND SERVICES

bakery/baker	αρτοποιείον/ψωμάς	artopiion/psomas
bank	τράπεζα	trapeza
barber	κουρέας	koureas
builder	κτίστης	ktistis
butcher	χασάπης	hassapis
cake shop	ζαχαροπλαστείο	zaharoplastio
camera shop	κατάστημα φωτογραφικών ειδών	katastima fotoghrafikon idhon
chemist (*person*)	φαρμακοποιός	farmakopios
(*shop*)	φαρμακείο	farmakio
dairy	γαλακτοπωλείον	ghalaktopolion
decorator	ελαιοχρωματιστής	eleohromatistis
dentist	οδοντογιατρός	odhondoghiatros
department store	κατάστημα	katastima

doctor	γιατρός	ghiatros
dry cleaners	στεγνοκαθαριστήριο	steghnokatharistirio
electrical appliances	ηλεκτρικές συσκευές	ilektrikes siskeves
electrician	ηλεκτρολόγος	ilektrologhos
grocer (*person*)	μπακάλης	bakalis
(*shop*)	μπακάλικο	bakaliko
greengrocer (*person*)	μανάβης	manavis
(*shop*)	μανάβικο	manaviko
hardware shop/ ironmonger	σιδεράς	sidheras
launderette/laundry	πλυντήριο	plintirio
market	αγορά	aghora
newsagent	εφημεριδοπώλης	efimeridhopolis
notary	συμβολαιογράφος	simvoleoghrafos
photographer	φωτογράφος	fotoghrafos
plumber	υδραυλικός	idhravlikos
police	αστυνομία	astinomia
post office	ταχυδρομείο	tahidhromio
shoe repairer	παπουτσής	papoutsis
sports shop	κατάστημα γιά είδη σπορ	katastima ghia idhi spor
stationer	χαρτοπωλείον	hartopolion
supermarket	υπεραγορά	iperaghora
sweet shop	ζαχαροπλαστείο	zaharoplastio
tobacconist	καπνοπωλείο	kapnopolio
toy shop	κατάστημα παιγνιδιών	katastima peghnidhion

| travel agent | γραφείο ταξιδίων | ghrafio taksidhion |
| wine merchant | έμπορος οίνων | emboros inon |

IN THE SHOP

Sale (clearance)	*Ξεπούλημα	Ksepoulima
Cash desk	*Ταμείο	Tamio
Shop assistant	Βοηθός	Voïthos
Manager	Διευθυντής	Dhiefthindis
Can I help you?	*Μπορώ να σας βοηθήσω;	Boro na sas voïthisso
I want to buy ...	Θέλω ν'αγοράσω ...	Thelo naghorasso
Do you sell ...?	Πουλάτε ...;	Poulate
I just want to look around	Θέλω μόνο να κοιτάξω	Thelo mono na kitaxo
I don't want to buy anything now	Δεν θέλω ν'αγοράσω τίποτα τώρα	Dhen thelo naghorasso tipota tora
I don't like this	Δεν μ'αρέσει	Dhen maressi
I'll have this	Θα πάρω αυτό	Tha paro afto
Could you show me ...?	Μπορείτε να μου δείξετε ...;	Borite na mou dhixete
We do not have it/that	*Δεν το έχουμε	Dhen to ehoume
We've sold out, but we'll have more tomorrow	*Δεν έχουμε άλλο, αλλά ελάτε αύριο πάλι	Dhen ehoume alo, ala elate avrio pali
Anything else?	*Τίποτα άλλο;	Tipota alo
That will be all, thank you	Τίποτα άλλο, ευχαριστώ	Tipota allo, efharisto

Will you take it with you?	*Θα το πάρετε μαζί σας;	Tha to parete mazi sas
I'll take it with me	Θα το πάρω μαζί μου	Tha to paro mazi mou
Please send them to this address/this hotel	Σας παρακαλώ στείλτε τα σ'αυτή τη διεύθυνση/ σ'αυτό το ξενοδοχείο	Sas parakalo stilte ta safti ti dhiefthinssi/safto to ksenodhohio

CHOOSING

I want something in leather/green	Θέλω κάτι δερμάτινο/σε πράσινο χρώμα	Thelo kati dhermatino/se prassino hroma
I need it to match this	Θέλω να ταιριάζη με αυτό	Thelo na teriazi me afto
I like the one in the window	Μ'αρέσει αυτό που είναι στη βιτρίνα	Maressi afto pou ine sti vitrina
Could I see that one, please?	Μπορώ να δω εκείνο παρακαλώ;	Boro na dho ekino parakalo
I like the colour but not the style	Μ'αρέσει το χρώμα αλλά όχι το στυλ	Maressi to hroma ala ohi to stil
I want a darker/lighter shade	Θέλω ένα πιό σκούρο/πιό ανοικτό χρώμα	Thelo ena pio skouro/pio anikto hroma
I need something warmer/thinner	Χρειάζομαι κάτι πιό ζεστό/πιό ψιλό	Hriazome kati pio zesto/ pio psilo
Do you have one in another colour/size?	Το έχετε σε άλλο χρώμα/μέγεθος;	To ehete se alo hroma/ meghethos

Have you anything better/cheaper?	Έχετε τίποτα καλύτερο/ φθηνότερο;	Ehete tipota kalitero/ fthinotero
How much is this?	Πόσο κάνει αυτό;	Posso kani afto
That is too much for me	Αυτό είναι πολύ γιά μένα	Afto ine poli ghia mena
What's it made of?	Από τί είναι;	Apo ti ine
Is there a mirror?	Έχετε ένα καθρέπτη;	Ehete ena kathrepti
Is it colour-fast?	Ξεβάφει;	Ksevafi
Is it machine-washable?	Πλένεται στο πλυντήριο;	Plenete sto plindirio
Will it shrink?	Θα μαζέψει;	Tha mazepsi
Is it handmade?	Είναι χειροποίητο;	Ine hiropiito
What size is this?	Τι μέγεθος είναι αυτό;	Ti meghethos ine afto
Have you a larger/ smaller one?	Έχετε ένα μεγαλύτερο/ μικρότερο;	Ehete ena meghalitero/ mikrotero
I take size[1] ...	Παίρνω μέγεθος ...	Perno meghethos
The English/American size is ...	Το Εγγλέζικο/ Αμερικάνικο μέγεθος είναι ...	To engleziko/amerikaniko meghethos ine
My collar/chest size is ...	Το μέγεθος του κολλάρου/στήθους μου είναι ...	To meghethos tou kolarou/stithous mou ine
My waist measurement is ...	Η μέση μου είναι ...	I messi mou ine

1. See p. 125 for table of continental sizes.

| Can I try it on? | Μπορώ να το δοκιμάσω; | Boro na to dhokimasso |
| It's too short/long/ tight/loose | Είναι πολύ κοντό/ μακρύ/στενό/ φαρδύ | Ine poli konto/makri/ steno/fardhi |

MATERIALS

cotton	βαμβακερό	vamvakero
lace	δαντέλα	dhantela
leather	δέρμα	dherma
linen	λινό	lino
plastic	πλαστικό	plastiko
silk	μεταξωτό	metaksoto
suede	σουέντ	suede
synthetic	συνθετικό	sinthetiko
wool	μάλλινο	malino

COLOURS

beige	μπέζ	beige
black	μαύρο	mavro
blue	μπλε	ble
brown	καφέ	kafe
gold	χρυσό	hrisso
green	πράσινο	prassino

grey	**γκρίζο**	grizo
mauve	**μωβ**	mauve
orange	**πορτοκαλί**	portokali
pink	**ροζ**	roz
purple	**βυσσινί**	vissini
red	**κόκκινο**	kokino
silver	**ασημένιο**	assimenio
white	**άσπρο**	aspro
yellow	**κίτρινο**	kitrino

COMPLAINTS

I want to see the manager	**Θέλω να δω τον διευθυντή**	Thelo na dho ton dhiefthindi
I bought this yesterday	**Τ'αγόρασα χθες**	Taghorassa hthes
I want to return this	**Θέλω να το επιστρέψω**	Thelo na to epistrepso
It doesn't work	**Δεν λειτουργεί**	Dhen litourghi
It does not fit	**Δεν χωράει**	Dhen horai

This is
  dirty
  stained
  torn
  broken
  cracked
	**Αυτό είναι
	  βρώμικο
	  λεκιασμένο
	  σκισμένο
	  σπασμένο
	  ραγισμένο**
		Afto ine
		  vromiko
		  lekiasmeno
		  skismeno
		  spasmeno
		  raghismeno

Will you change it, please?	**Μου τ'αλλάζετε παρακαλώ;**	Mou talazete parakalo

| Will you refund my money? | Θα μου επιστρέψετε τα χρήματα μου; | Tha mou epistrepsete ta hrimata mou |
| Here is the receipt | Να η απόδειξη | Na i apodhiksi |

PAYING

How much is this?	Πόσο κάνει αυτό;	Posso kani afto
That's ... please	*Αυτό είναι ... παρακαλώ	Afto ine ... parakalo
They are ... each	*Αυτά κάνουν ... το ένα	Afta kanoun ... to ena
How much does that come to?	Στα πόσα έρχεται;	Sta possa erhete
Will you take English/ American currency?	Παίρνετε Αγγλικά/ Αμερικάνικα χρήματα;	Pernete anglika/ amerikanika hrimata
Do you take travellers' cheques?	Παίρνετε τράβελλερς τσέκς;	Pernete travellers' cheques
Please pay the cashier	Πληρώστε στο ταμείο παρακαλώ	Pliroste sto tamio parakalo
May I have a receipt, please?	Μου δίνετε μία απόδειξη παρακαλώ;	Mou dhinete mia apodhiksi parakalo
You've given me too little/too much change	Μου δώσατε λιγότερα/ περισσότερα ρέστα	Mou dhossate lighotera/ perissotera resta
Do I have to pay VAT?	Είμαι υποχρεωμένος να πληρώσω φόρο;	Ime ipohreomenos na plirosso foro

CHEMIST

Can you prepare this prescription for me, please?	Μου ετοιμάζετε αυτή τη συνταγή παρακαλώ;	Mou etimazete afti ti sintaghi parakalo
Have you a small first aid kit?	Έχετε ένα μικρό κουτί με πρώτες βοήθειες;	Ehete ena mikro kouti me protes voithies
I want some aspirin/ sun cream for children	Θέλω μερικές ασπιρίνες/κρέμα ηλίου για παιδιά	Thelo merikes aspirines/ krema iliou ghia pedhia
Adhesive plaster	Λευκοπλάστη	Lefkoplasti
Can you suggest something for indigestion? constipation? diarrhoea?	Τί θα μου συστήνατε για δυσπεψία; δυσκοιλιότητα; διάρρεια;	Ti tha mou sistinate ghia dhispepsia dhiskiliotita dhiaria
I want an antiseptic cream	Θέλω μιά αντισυπτική κρέμα	Thelo mia antissiptiki krema
a disinfectant a mouthwash	ένα αντισυπτικό ένα αντισυπτικό για το στόμα	ena antissiptiko ena antissiptiko ghia to stoma
some nose drops	σταγόνες μύτης	staghones mitis
Do you sell contraceptives?	Πουλάτε προφυλακτικά;	Poulate profilaktika
Can you give me something for sunburn?	Μου δίνετε κάτι για κάψιμο από τον ήλιο;	Mou dhinete kati ghia kapsimo apo ton ilio

I want some	Θέλω	Thelo
throat lozenges	παστίλιες γιά το λαιμό	pastilles ghia to lemo
antiseptic cream	αντισηπτική κρέμα	antissiptiki krema
lipsalve	αλοιφή γιά τα χείλια	alifi ghia ta hilia
Do you have	Έχετε	Ehete
sanitary towels?	πετσέτες υγείας;	petsetes ighias
tampons?	ταμπόνς;	tampons
cotton wool?	βαμβάκι;	vamvaki
I need something for insect bites/travel sickness	Χρειάζομαι κάτι γιά τσιμπήματα εντόμων/ναυτία	Hriazome kati ghia tsimbimata endomon/naftia

TOILET ARTICLES

A packet of razor blades, please	Ένα κουτάκι ξυράφια παρακαλώ	Ena koutaki ksirafia parakalo
Have you an after-shave lotion?	Έχετε καμιά λοσιόν γιά μετά το ξύρισμα;	Ehete kamia lossion ghia meta to ksirisma
A tube of toothpaste, please	Μία οδοντόπαστα παρακαλώ	Mia odhontopasta parakalo
A box of paper handkerchiefs, please	Ένα κουτί με χαρτομάντηλα παρακαλώ	Ena kouti me hartomandila parakalo
A roll of toilet paper, please	Ένα ρολό χαρτί τουαλέτας παρακαλώ	Ena rolo harti toualetas parakalo

I'd like some cleansing cream/ lotion	Θέλω μιά κρέμα καθαρισμου προσώπου/λοσιόν γιά καθάρισμα	Thelo mia krema katharismou prossopou/losion ghia katharisma
hand cream	κρέμα γιά τα χέρια	krema ghia ta heria
lipsalve	κρέμα γιά τα χείλια	krema ghia ta hilia

CLOTHES AND SHOES[1]

I want a (sun) hat	Θέλω ένα (γιά τον ήλιο) καπέλλο	Thelo ena (ghia ton ilio) kapelo
I'd like a pair of gloves	Θέλω ένα ζευγάρι γάντια	Thelo ena zevghari ghantia
Can I look at some dresses, please?	Μπορώ να δω μερικά φορέματα παρακαλώ;	Boro na dho merika foremata parakalo
Where can I find socks/stockings?	Που θα βρω κάλτσες ανδρικές/ γυναικείες;	Pou tha vro kaltses andrikes/ghinekies
I am looking for a blouse bra jumper	Ψάχνω γιά μπλούζα σουτιέν πουλόβερ	Psahno ghia blouza soutien poulover
I need a coat/jacket	Χρειάζομαι ένα παλτό/σακάκι	Hriazome ena palto/ sakaki

1. For sizes, see p. 125.

Do you sell buttons? elastic? zips?	Πουλάτε κουμπιά; ελαστική ταινία; φερμουάρ;	Poulate koumbia elastiki tenia fermouar
Where are beach clothes?	Που είναι τα ρούχα γιά την πλαζ;	Pou ine ta rouha ghia tin plaz
I want a short/long sleeved shirt, collar size ...	Θέλω ένα πουκάμισο με κοντά/μακρυά μανίκια, μέγεθος ...	Thelo ena poukamisso me konta/makria manikia, meghethos
I need a pair of walking shoes	Χρειάζομαι ένα ζευγάρι γερά παπούτσια	Hriazome ena zevghari ghera papoutsia
I need a pair of beach sandals/black shoes	Χρειάζομαι ένα ζευγάρι σανδάλια/ μαύρα παπούτσια	Hriazome ena zevghari sandhalia/mavra papoutsia
These heels are too high/too low	Αυτά τα τακούνια είναι πολύ ψηλά/ χαμηλά	Afta ta takounia ine poli psila/hamila
This doesn't fit	Δεν μου χωράει	Dhen mou horai
I don't know the Greek size	Δεν ξέρω το ελληνικό μέγεθος	Dhen ksero to elliniko meghethos
Can you measure me?	Μπορείτε να με μετρήσετε;	Borite na me metrissete
It's for a 3-year-old	Είναι γιά ένα παιδάκι τριών χρονών	Ine ghia ena pedhaki trion hronon

CLOTHING SIZES[1]

WOMEN'S DRESSES, ETC

British	10	12	14	16	18	20
American	8	10	12	14	16	18
Continental	30	32	34	36	38	40

MEN'S SUITS

British and American	36	38	40	42	44	46
Continental	46	48	50	52	54	56

MEN'S SHIRTS

British and American	14	$14\frac{1}{2}$	15	$15\frac{1}{2}$	16	$16\frac{1}{2}$	17
Continental	36	37	38	39	41	42	43

STOCKINGS

British and American	8	$8\frac{1}{2}$	9	$9\frac{1}{2}$	10	$10\frac{1}{2}$	11
Continental	0	1	2	3	4	5	6

SOCKS

British and American	$9\frac{1}{2}$	10	$10\frac{1}{2}$	11	$11\frac{1}{2}$
Continental	38–39	39–40	40–41	41–42	42–43

1. This table is only intended as a rough guide, since sizes vary from manufacturer to manufacturer.

SHOES

British	1	2	3	4	5	6	7	8	9	10	11	12
American	2½	3½	4½	5½	6½	7½	8½	9½	10½	11½	12½	13½
Continental	33	34–5	36	37	38	39–40	41	42	43	44	45	46

FOOD[1]

Give me a kilo/half a kilo of ..., please	Δώστε μου ένα κιλό/ μισό κιλό ..., παρακαλώ	Dhoste mou ena kilo/ misso kilo ..., parakalo
I want some sweets/ chocolate	Θέλω λίγα γλυκά/ λίγη σοκολάτα	Thelo ligha ghlika/lighi sokolata
A bottle of milk/beer	Ένα μπουκάλι γάλα/μπύρα	Ena boukali ghala/bira
Is there anything back on the bottle?	Επιστρέφεται τίποτα γιά το μπουκάλι;	Epistrefete tipota ghia to boukali
I want a jar/tin/packet of ...	Θέλω ένα βάζο/μία κονσέρβα/ένα πακέτο ...	Thelo ena vazo/mia konserva/ena paketo
How much a kilo/ bottle?	Πόσο το κιλό/ μπουκάλι;	Posso to kilo/boukali
A loaf of bread	Μία φραντζόλα ψωμί	Mia frandzola psomi

1. See also the various MENU sections (pp. 100) and WEIGHTS AND MEASURES (pp. 196–200).

Do you sell frozen foods?	Πουλάτε κατεψυγμένα τρόφιμα;	Poulate katepsighmena trofima
These pears are too hard/soft	Αυτά τ'αχλάδια είναι πολύ σκληρά/ μαλακά	Afta tahladhia ine poli sklira/malaka
... slices of ham please	... φέτες ζαμπόν παρακαλώ	... fetes zambon parakalo
Is it fresh or frozen?	Είναι φρέσκο ή παγωμένο;	Ine fresko i paghomeno
Are they ripe?	Είναι γινομένα;	Ine ghinomena
This is bad/stale	Είναι χαλασμένο/ μπαγιάτικο	Ine halasmeno/baghiatiko
Will you mince it/bone it?	Μου το κάνετε κιμά/ ξεκοκκαλιάζετε;	Mou to kanete kima/ ksekokaliazete
Will you clean the fish?	Θα μου καθαρίσετε το ψάρι;	Tha mou katharisete to psari
Leave/take off the head	Αφήστε/αφαιρέστε το κεφάλι	Afiste/afereste to kefali
Please fillet the fish	Σας παρακαλώ κόψτε το ψάρι σε φιλέτα	Sas parakalo kopste to psari se fileta
Is there any shellfish?	Έχετε θαλασσινά;	Ehete thalassina
Shall I help myself?	Να πάρω μόνος/-η μου;	Na paro monos/-i mou

HAIRDRESSER AND BARBER

May I make an appointment for tomorrow/this afternoon?	Μπορώ να κλείσω ένα ραντεβού γιά αύριο/σήμερα τ'απόγευμα;	Boro na klisso ena rendezvous ghia avrio/simera tapoghevma
What time?	*Τι ώρα;	Ti ora
I want my hair cut (trimmed)	Θέλω να μου κόψετε τα μαλλιά (λίγο)	Thelo na mou kopsete ta malia (ligho)
Not too short at the sides	Οχι πολύ κοντά στο πλάι	Ohi poli konta sto plai
I'll have it shorter at the back/on top	Λίγο πιό κοντά από πίσω/επάνω	Ligho pio konta apo pisso/epano
No shorter	Όχι πιό κοντά	Ohi pio konda
My hair is oily/dry	Τα μαλλιά μου είναι λιπαρά/ξηρά	Ta malia mou ine lipara/ksira
I want a shampoo	Θέλω λούσιμο	Thelo loussimo
Please use conditioner	Σας παρακαλώ να μου βάλετε κοντίτιονερ	Sas parakalo na mou valete konditioner
I want my hair washed, styled and blow-dried	Θέλω να μου πλύνετε τα μαλλιά μου, να τα χτενίσετε και να τα στεγνώσετε	Thelo na mou plinete ta malia mou, na ta ktenissete ke na ta steghnossete
I want a perm	Θέλω να μου κάνετε περμανάντ	Thelo na mou kanete permanant
Have you any lacquer?	Έχετε λάκκα;	Ehete laka

Please do not use any hairspray	**Παρακαλώ μη χρησιμοποιήσετε σπρέι**	Parakalo mi hrissimopiissete spray
The water is too cold	**Το νερό είναι πολύ κρύο**	To nero ine poli krio
The dryer is too hot	**Το σεσουάρ είναι πολύ ζεστό**	To sesouar ine poli zesto
That's fine	**Εντάξει**	Entaksi
Thank you, I like it very much	**Ευχαριστώ, μ'αρέσει πάρα πολύ**	Efharisto, maressi para poli
I want a shave/ manicure	**Θέλω να με ξυρίσετε/μανικιούρ**	Thelo na me ksirissete/ manikiour
Shave and hair cut	**Ξύρισμα και κούρεμα**	Ksirisma ke kourema
Please trim my beard/ my moustache	**Σας παρακαλώ κόψτε λίγο το γένι μου/το μουστάκι μου**	Sas parakalo kopste ligho to gheni mou/to moustaki mou

HARDWARE[1]

Do you have a battery for this?	**Έχετε μπαταρία γι'αυτό;**	Ehete bataria ghiafto
Where can I get butane gas/paraffin?	**Που μπορώ να βρώ μπουκάλα γιά το γκάζι/παραφίνη;**	Pou boro na vro boukala ghia to gazi/parafini

1. See also CAMPING, p. 66.

I need	Χρειάζομαι ένα	Hriazome ena
corkscrew	τιρμπουσόν	tirbouson
can/bottle-opener	ανοιχτήρι	aniktiri
a small/large	μικρό/μεγάλο	mikro/meghalo
screwdriver	κατσαβίδι	katsavidhi

| I'd like some candles/ matches | Θέλω μερικά κεριά/ σπίρτα | Thelo merika keria/spirta |

| I want a torch/pen knife/pair of scissors | Θέλω ένα φακό/ σουγιά/ψαλίδι | Thelo ena fako/soughia/ psalidhi |

| Do you sell any string/rope? | Πουλάτε σπάγγο/ σκοινί; | Poulate spango/skini |

Where can I find	Που μπορώ να βρώ	Pou boro na vro
washing-up liquid?	υγρό γιά τα πιάτα;	ighro ghia ta piata
scouring powder?	Βιμ;	Vim
soap pads?	σύρμα;	sirma

| Do you have a dishcloth/brush? | Έχετε σφουγγάρι γιά τα πιάτα/βούρτσα; | Ehete sfoungari ghia ta piata/vourtsa |

I need	Χρειάζομαι	Hriazome
a groundsheet	ένα αδιάβροχο σεντόνι	ena adhiavroho sendoni
a bucket	έναν κουβά	enan kouva
a frying pan	ένα τηγάνι	ena tighani

| I want to buy a barbecue | Θέλω ν'αγοράσω μιά ψησταριά | Thelo naghorasso mia psistaria |

| Do you sell charcoal? | Πουλάτε κάρβουνα; | Poulate karvouna |

| adaptor | μετασχηματιστής | metaskhimatistis |

| basket | καλάθι | kalathi |

| duster | ξεσκονόπανο | kseskonopano |

| electrical flex | ηλεκτρικό καλώδιο | ilektriko kalodhio |

extension lead	επιμηκυντικό καλώδιο	epimikindiko kalodhio
fuse	ασφάλεια	asfalia
fuse wire	σύρμα γιά ασφάλεια	sirma ghia asfalia
insulating tape	μονωτική ταινία	monotiki tenia
light bulb	λάμπα	lamba
penknife	σουγιάς	soughias
plug (*bath*)	βούλωμα μπανιέρας	vouloma banieras
plug (*electrical*)	πρίζα	priza

LAUNDRY AND DRY CLEANING

Where is the nearest launderette/dry cleaner?	Που είναι το πλησιέστερο πλυντήριο/ στεγνοκαθαριστήριο;	Pou ine to plissiestero plintirio/ steghnokatharistirio
I want to have these things washed/ cleaned	Θέλω να μου πλύνετε αυτά/καθαρίσετε αυτά	Thelo na mou plinete afta/katharissete afta
These stains won't come out	*Αυτοί οι λεκέδες δεν βγαίνουν	Afti i lekedhes dhen vghenoun
Can you get this stain out?	Μπορείτε να βγάλετε αυτόν τον λεκέ;	Borite na vgalete afton ton leke
It is coffee wine grease	Είναι από καφέ κρασί λίπος	Ine apo kafe krassi lipos
It only needs to be pressed	Χρειάζεται μόνο σιδέρωμα	Hriazete mono sidheroma

This is torn. Can you mend it?	Αυτό έχει σκιστεί. Μπορείτε να το μπαλώσετε;	Afto ehi skisti. Borite na to balossete
There's a button missing	Λείπει ένα κουμπί	Lipi ena koumbi
Can you sew on a button?	Μου ράβετε ένα κουμπί;	Mou ravete ena koumbi
Can you put in a new zip?	Μου βάζετε ένα καινούργιο φερμουάρ;	Mou vazete ena kenourghio fermouar
When will they be ready?	Πότε θα είναι έτοιμα;	Pote tha in' etima
I need them by this evening/tomorrow	Τα χρειάζομαι απόψε/αύριο	Ta hriazome apopse/avrio
Call back at 5 o'clock	*Γυρίστε στις πέντε τ'απόγευμα	Ghiriste stis pente tapoghevma
We can do it by Thursday	*Μπορούμε να το έχουμε έτοιμο την Πέμπτη	Boroume na to ehoume etimo tin pempti
It will take three days	*Θα πάρει τρεις μέρες	Tha pari tris meres
This isn't mine	Αυτό δεν είναι δικό μου	Afto dhen ine dhiko mou
I've lost my ticket	Έχασα την απόδειξη μου	Ehassa tin apodhiksi mou

HOUSEHOLD LAUNDRY

bath towel	πετσέτα μπάνιου	petseta baniou
blanket	κουβέρτα	kouverta

napkin	**πετσέτα**	petseta
pillow case	**μαξιλαροθήκη**	maksilarothiki
sheet	**σεντόνι**	sendoni
tablecloth	**τραπεζομάντηλο**	trapezomandilo
towel (tea)	**πετσέτα (πιάτων)**	petseta (piaton)

NEWSPAPERS, BOOKS AND WRITING MATERIALS

Do you sell English/ American newspapers?	**Έχετε Αγγλικές/ Αμερικανικές εφημερίδες;**	Ehete anglikes/ amerikanikes efimeridhes
Can you get this magazine for me?	**Μπορείτε να μου παραγγείλετε αυτό το περιοδικό;**	Borite na mou parangilete afto to periodhiko
Where can I get the ...?	**Που μπορώ να βρω το ...;**	Pou boro na vro to
I want a map of the city	**Θέλω ένα χάρτη της πόλης**	Thelo ena harti tis polis
I want a road map of ...	**Θέλω έναν οδικό χάρτη του**	Thelo enan odhiko harti tou
Do you have any English books?	**Έχετε Αγγλικά βιβλία;**	Ehete anglika vivlia
Have you any novels by ...?	**Έχετε τίποτα μυθιστορήματα του ...;**	Ehete tipota mithistorimata tou
I want some postcards	**Θέλω μερικές καρτ- ποστάλ**	Thelo merikes kartpostal

Do you sell souvenirs/toys at all?	Πουλάτε τίποτα σουβενίρ/ παιγνίδια;	Poulate tipota souvenir/ peghnidhia
ballpoint	μπικ	bic
calculator	υπολογιστική μηχανή	ipologhistiki mihani
card	κάρτα	karta
dictionary	λεξικό	lexiko
drawing paper	χαρτί σχεδίου	harti skhedhiou
drawing pin	πινέζα	pineza
elastic band	λαστιχάκι	lastihaki
envelope	φάκελλος	fakelos
felt-tip pen	μαλακιά πέννα	malakia pena
fountain pen	στυλό	stilo
glue	κόλλα	kola
guide book	τουριστικός οδηγός	touristikos odhighos
ink	μελάνι	melani
notebook	σημειωματάριο	simiomatario
paper	χαρτί	harti
paperclip	συνδετήρας	sindhetiras
pen	πέννα	pena
pen cartridge	φυσίγγιο μελάνης πέννας	fissingio melanis penas
pencil	μολύβι	molivi
pencil sharpener	ξύστρα	ksistra
postcard	καρτ-ποστάλ	kartpostal
rubber	γόμμα	ghoma

sellotape	σελλοτέιπ	sellotape
string	σπάγγος	spangos
writing paper	χαρτί αλληλογραφίας	harti aliloghrafias

PHOTOGRAPHY

I want to buy a (cine) camera	Θέλω ν'αγοράσω μιά (κινηματογραφική) μηχανή	Thelo naghorasso mia (kinimatoghrafiki) mihani
Have you a film/ cartridge for this camera?	Έχετε φίλμ/κασέτα γι'αυτή τη μηχανή;	Ehete film/kasseta ghiafti ti mihani
Can I have a 35mm film?	Μπορώ να έχω ένα φίλμ των τριανταπέντε μιλιμέτρ;	Boro na eho ena film ton triantapende milimetre
20/36 exposures	Είκοσι/τριανταέξη εμφανίσεις	Ikossi/triantaeksi emfanissis
A 100/400/1000 ASA film please	Ένα φίλμ εκατό/ τετρακοσίων/ χιλίων ασα παρακαλώ	Ena film ekato/ tetrakossion/hilion ASA parakalo
What is the fastest film you have?	Ποιό είναι το πιό ταχύ φίλμ που έχετε;	Pio ine to pio tahi film pou ehete
Film for slides/prints	Φίλμ γιά διαφάνεια/ φωτογραφίες	Film ghia dhiafania/ fotoghrafies

I want a (fast) colour film/black-and-white film	Θέλω ένα φίλμ (υψηλής ταχύτητος) γιά έγχρωμες/ασπρό-μαυρες φωτογραφίες	Thelo ena film (ipsilis tahititos) ghia enhromes/aspro-mavres fotoghrafies
Would you fit the film in the camera for me, please?	Μου βάζετε το φίλμ στη μηχανή μου σας παρακαλώ;	Mou vazete to film sti mihani mou sas parakalo
How much is it?	Πόσο κάνει;	Posso kani
Does the price include processing?	Συμπεριλαμβάνεται η εμφάνιση στη τιμή;	Simberilamvanete i emfanissi sti timi
Do you have flash bulbs/cubes?	Έχετε φλάς;	Ehete flas
I'd like this film developed and printed	Θέλω να μου εμφανίσετε αυτό το φίλμ	Thelo na mou emfanissete afto to film
Can I have ... prints/ enlargements of this negative?	Μπορώ να έχω ... αντίτυπα/μεγεθύνσεις από αυτό το αρνητικό;	Boro na eho ... anditipa/meghethinssis apo afto to arnitiko
When will they be ready?	Πότε θα είναι έτοιμες;	Pote tha ine etimes
Will they be done tomorrow?	Θα είναι έτοιμες αύριο;	Tha ine etimes avrio
My camera's not working. Can you mend it?	Η μηχανή μου δεν λειτουργεί. Μπορείτε να μου την επιδιορθώσετε;	I mihani mou dhen litourghi. Borite na mou tin epidhiorthossete

There is something the matter with the shutter	Κάτι συμβαίνει με τον φωτοφράκτη	Kati simveni me ton fotofrakti
the light meter	το φωτόμετρο	to fotometro
the film winder	το κλειδί κουρδίσματος του φίλμ	to klidhi kourdhismatos tou film
The film is jammed	Έχει πιάσει το φίλμ	Ehi piassi to film
I need a (haze) filter	Χρειάζομαι ένα φίλτρο (συσκοτίσεως)	Hriazome ena filtro (siskotisseos)
battery	μπαταρία	bataria
cine film	φίλμ κινηματογραφικής μηχανής	film kinimatoghrafikis mihanis
filter	φίλτρο	filtro
lens	φακός	fakos
lens cap	καπάκι φακού	kapaki fakou
light meter	φωτόμετρο	fotometro
video camera	μηχανή γιά βίντεο	mihani ghia video

RECORDS AND CASSETTES

| Do you have any records/cassettes of local music? | Έχετε δίσκους/ κασέττες ντόπιας μουσικής; | Ehete dhiskous/kassetes dopias moussikis |
| Are there any new records by ...? | Έχετε νέους δίσκους του ...; | Ehete neous dhiskous tou |

Do you sell compact discs/video cassettes?	Πουλάτε κόμπακτ δίσκους/ βίντεοκασέττες;	Poulate kompakt dhiskous/videokassetes
Can I listen to this record, please?	Μπορώ ν'ακούσω αυτόν τον δίσκο παρακαλώ;	Boro nakousso afton ton dhisko parakalo

TOBACCONIST

Do you stock English/ American cigarettes?	Έχετε Αγγλικά/ Αμερικανικά τσιγάρα;	Ehete anglika/amerikanika tsighara
A packet of ...	Ένα κουτί ...	Ena kouti
I want some cigarettes with/without filter	Θέλω τσιγάρα με/ χωρίς φίλτρο	Thelo tsighara me/horis filtro
A box of large/small cigars	Ένα κουτί με μεγάλα/μικρά πούρα	Ena kouti me meghala/ mikra poura
I'd like some dark/light tobacco	Θέλω λίγο μαύρο/ ξανθό καπνό	Thelo ligho mavro/ ksantho kapno
A box of matches	Ένα κουτί σπίρτα	Ena kouti spirta
Do you have cigarette papers/pipe cleaners?	Έχετε τσιγαρόχαρτο/ καθαριστήρες γιά πίπες;	Ehete tsigharoharto/ katharistires ghia pipes
I want to buy a lighter	Θέλω ν'αγοράσω έναν αναπτήρα	Thelo naghorasso enan anaptira
Do you sell lighter fuel/flints?	Έχετε βενζίνη/πέτρες γι'αναπτήρες;	Ehete venzini/petres ghianaptires

| I want a gas refill for this lighter | Θέλω ένα ανταλλακτικό με αέριο γ'αυτόν τον αναπτήρα | Thelo ena antalaktiko me aerio ghiafton ton anaptira |

REPAIRS

This is broken. Could somebody mend it?	Είναι σπασμένο. Μπορεί κανείς να το επιδιορθώσει;	Ine spasmeno. bori kanis na to epidhiorthossi
Can you sole these shoes (with leather)?	Μπορείτε να μου βάλετε (δερμάτινες) σόλες;	Borite na mou valete (dhermatines) soles
Can you heel these shoes (with rubber)?	Μπορείτε να μου βάλετε (λαστιχένια) τακούνια;	Borite na mou valete (lastihenia) takounia
I have broken the heel. Can you put on a new one?	Έσπασα το τακούνι. Μου βάζετε ένα καινούργιο;	Espassa to takouni. Mou vazete ena kenourghio
My watch is broken	Έσπασα το ρολόι μου	Espassa to roloi mou
Could you do it while I wait?	Θα μπορούσατε να το κάνετε καθώς θα περιμένω;	Tha borousate na to kanete kathos tha perimeno
When should I come back for it?	Πότε μπορώ να επιστρέψω γιά να το πάρω;	Pote boro na epistrepso ghia na to paro

I have broken the	Έσπασα το	Espassa to
glass	γυαλί	ghiali
strap	λουρί	louri
spring	ελατήριο	elatirio

I have broken	Έσπασα	Espassa
my glasses	τα γυαλιά μου	ta ghialia mou
the frame	τον σκελετό	ton skeleto
the arm	το χέρι	to heri

| How much would a new one cost? | Πόσο θα στοιχίση ένα καινούργιο; | Posso tha stihissi ena kenourghio |

| The stone/charm/ screw has come loose | Η πέτρα/το μπρελόκ/η βίδα έχει χαλαρώσει | I petra/to breloc/i vidha ehi halarossi |

| The fastener/clip/ chain is broken | Το κούμπωμα/η πόρπη/η αλυσίδα έχει σπάσει | To kouboma/i porpi/i alissidha ehi spassi |

| It can't be repaired | *Δεν διορθώνεται | Dhen dhiorthonete |

| You need a new one | *Χρειάζεστε ένα καινούργιο | Hriazeste ena kenourghio |

POST OFFICE

Where's the main post office?	Που είναι το κεντρικό ταχυδρομείο;	Pou ine to kendriko tahidhromio
Where's the nearest post office?	Που είναι το πλησιέστερο ταχυδρομείο;	Pou ine to plissiestero tahidhromio
What time does the post office close/open?	Τι ώρα κλείνει/ανοίγει το ταχυδρομείο;	Ti ora klini/anighi to tahidhromio
Where's the post box?	Που είναι το γραμματοκιβώτιο;	Pou ine to ghramatokivotio
Which window do I go to for	Σε πιά θυρίδα πρέπει να πάω γιά	Se pia thiridha prepi na pao ghia
stamps?	γραμματόσημα;	ghramatossima
telegrams?	τηλεγραφήματα;	tileghrafimata
money orders?	εντάλματα;	entalmata

LETTERS AND TELEGRAMS

How much is a letter to England?	Πόσο κάνει ένα γράμμα γιά την Αγγλία;	Posso kani ena ghrama ghia tin anglia
What's the airmail/ surface mail to the U.S.A.?	Πόσο κάνει ένα αεροπορικό/απλό γράμμα γιά την Αμερική;	Posso kani ena aeroporiko/aplo ghramma ghia tin ameriki
It's inland	Είναι εσωτερικού	Ine essoterikou
Give me three ... drahma stamps, please	Δώστε μου τρία γραμματόσημα των ... δραχμών	Dhoste mou tria ghramatossima ton ... dhrahmon
I want to send this letter express	Θέλω να στείλω αυτό το γράμμα κατεπείγον	Thelo na stilo afto to ghrama katepighon
I want to register this letter	Θέλω να στείλω αυτό το γράμμα συστημένο	Thelo na stilo afto to ghrama sistimeno
Two airmail forms	Δύο αεροπορικά έντυπα	Dhio aeroporika entipa
Where is the poste restante section?	Που είναι το πόστ-ρεστάντ	Pou ine to post restant
Are there any letters for me?	Έχετε γράμματα γιά μένα;	Ehete ghramata ghia mena
What is your name?	*Πώς λέγεστε;	Pos legheste
Have you any means of identification?	*Έχετε ταυτότητα;	Ehete taftotita

I want to send a telegram (reply paid)	Θέλω να στείλω ένα τηλεγράφημα (με πληρωμένη απάντηση)	Thelo na stilo ena tileghrafima (me pliromeni apantissi)
How much does it cost per word?	Πόσο κάνει η λέξη;	Posso kani i leksi
Write the message here and your own name and address	*Γράψτε το μύνημα εδώ και το όνομα και τή διεύθυνση σας	Ghrapste to minima edho ke tonoma ke ti dhiefthinssi sas
Can I send a telex?	Μπορώ να στείλω ένα τέλεξ;	Boro na stilo ena telex
I want to send a parcel	Θέλω να στείλω ένα δέμα	Thelo na stilo ena dhema

TELEPHONING

Where's the nearest phone box?	Που είναι ο πλησιέστερος τηλεφωνικός θάλαμος;	Pou ine o plissiesteros tilefonikos thalamos
I want to make a phone call	Θέλω να κάνω ένα τηλεφώνημα	Thelo na kano ena tilefonima
May I use your phone?	Μπορώ να χρησιμοποιήσω το τηλέφωνο σας;	Boro na hrissimopiisso to tilefono sas
Do you have a telephone directory for ...?	Έχετε τηλεφωνικό κατάλογο γιά ...;	Ehete tilefoniko katalogho ghia

Please give me a token	Δώστε μου μία τηλεφωνική μάρκα	Dhoste mou mia tilefoniki marka
Please get me ...	Σας παρακαλώ πάρτε μου ...	Sas parakalo parte mou
I want to telephone to England	Θέλω να τηλεφωνήσω στην Αγγλία	Thelo na tilefonisso stin anglia
I want to make a personal (person-to-person) call	Θέλω να κάνω ένα προσωπικό τηλεφώνημα	Thelo na kano ena prossopiko tilefonima
I want to reverse the charges (call collect)	Θέλω να χρεωθή το τηλεφώνημα (στον παραλήπτη)	Thelo na hreothi to tilefonima (ston paralipti)
Could you give me the cost (time and charges) afterwards?	Μου λέτε μετά πόσο είναι; πόση ώρ	Mou lete meta posso ine reonete
I was cut off. Can you reconnect me?	Με διέκοψαν. Μπορείτε να με επανασυνδέσετε;	Me dhiekopsan. Borite na me epanassindhessete
Hello	Εμπρός	Embros
I want extension 43	Θέλω εσωτερικό σαραντατρία	Thelo essoteriko sarantatria
May I speak to ...?	Μπορώ να μιλήσω στον ...;	Boro na milisso ston
Who's speaking?	*Ποιός μιλάει;	Pios milai
Hold the line, please	*Περιμένετε παρακαλώ	Perimenete parakalo
Put the receiver down	*Κατεβάστε το ακουστικό	Katevaste to akoustiko

He's not here	*Δεν είναι εδώ	Dhen ine edho
He's at ...	*Είναι στο ...	Ine sto
When will he be back?	Πότε θα επιστρέψη;	Pote tha epistrepsi
Will you take a message?	Μπορείτε να πάρετε μία παραγγελία;	Borite na parete mia parangelia
Tell him that ... phoned	Πέστε του ότι τηλεφώνησε ο ...	Peste tou oti tilefonisse o
Please ask him to phone me	Πέστε του σας παρακαλώ να μου τηλεφωνήση	Peste tou sas parakalo na mou tilefonissi
What's your number?	*Ποιός είναι ο αριθμός σας;	Pios ine o arithmos sas
My number is ...	Ο αριθμός μου είναι ...	O arithmos mou ine
I can't hear you	Δεν σας ακούω	Dhen sas akouo
The line is engaged	*Η γραμμή είναι κατειλημμένη	I ghrami ine katilimeni
The number is out of order	*Το τηλέφωνο δεν λειτουργεί	To tilefono dhen litourghi
There's no reply	*Δεν απαντάει κανείς	Dhen apantai kanis
You haven't got the right number	*Δεν έχετε τον σωστό αριθμό	Dhen ehete ton sosto arithmo
Telephone directory	Τηλεφωνικός κατάλογος	Tilefonikos kataloghos
Telephone number	Αριθμός τηλεφώνου	Arithmos tilefonou
Telephone operator	Τηλεφωνητής (masc.) τηλεφωνήτρια (fem.)	Tilefonitis/tilefonitria

What do I dial to get the international operator?	**Τι παίρνω γιά το τηλεφωνικό κέντρο εξωτερικού γραμμών;**	Ti perno ghia to tilefoniko kendro eksoterikou ghramon
What is the code for ...?	**Ποιός είναι ο κωδικός αριθμός γιά ...;**	Pios ine o kodhikos arithmos ghia
Can I dial direct to ...?	**Μπορώ να παρω κατευθείαν ...;**	boro na paro katefthian
How much does a call cost?	**Πόσο κάνει;**	Posso kani

SIGHTSEEING

Where is the tourist office?	Που είναι το γραφείο τουρισμού;	Pou ine to ghrafio tourismou
What should we see here?	Τι πρέπει να δούμε εδώ;	Ti prepi na dhoume edho
Is there a map/plan of the places to visit?	Υπάρχει χάρτης/ σχεδιάγραμμα των τοποθεσιών που πρέπει να επισκεφτούμε;	Iparhi hartis/ skhedhiagrama ton topothession pou prepi na episkeftoume
I want a good guidebook	Θέλω ένα καλό οδηγό	Thelo ena kalo odhigho
Is there a good sightseeing tour?	Υπάρχει κανένα καλό τούρ των αξιοθεάτων;	Iparhi kanena kalo tour ton aksiotheaton
Does the bus stop at the ... Hotel?	Σταματάει το λεωφορείο στο Ξενοδοχείο ...;	Stamatai to leoforio sto ksenodhohio

Is there an excursion to …?	Υπάρχει εκδρομή γιά το …;	Iparhi ekdhromi ghia to
How long does the tour take?	Πόση ώρα παίρνει το τούρ;	Possi ora perni to tour
Are there guided tours of the museum?	Υπάρχουν τούρ με ξεναγούς στο μουσείο;	Iparhoun tour me ksenaghous sto moussio
Does the guide speak English?	Μιλάει αγγλικά ο ξεναγός;	Milai anglika o ksenaghos
We don't need a guide	Δεν χρειαζόμαστε ξεναγό	Dhen hriazomaste ksenagho
I would prefer to go round alone; is that all right?	Προτιμώ να τριγυρίσω μόνος/-η μου, σας πειράζει;	Protimo na trighirisso monos/-i mou, sas pirazi
How much does the tour cost?	Πόσο κοστίζει το τούρ;	Posso kostizi to tour
Are all admission fees included?	Τα εισιτήρια συμπεριλαμβάνονται;	Ta issitiria siberilamvanonte
Does it include lunch?	Συμπεριλαμβάνει το μεσημεριανό φαγητό;	Siberilamvani to messimeriano faghito

MUSEUMS AND ART GALLERIES

| When does the museum open/ close? | Τι ώρα ανοίγει/ κλείνει το μουσείο; | Ti ora anighi/klini to moussio |
| Is it open every day? | Είναι ανοικτό κάθε μέρα; | Ine anikto kathe mera |

The gallery is closed on Mondays	*Η γαλαρία είναι κλειστή τις Δευτέρες	I halaria ine klisti tis dhefteres
How much does it cost?	Πόσο κάνει;	Posso kani
Are there reductions for children? students? the elderly?	Υπάρχουν μειωμένες τιμές γιά τα παιδιά; τους φοιτητές; τους ηλικιωμένους;	Iparhoun miomenes times ghia ta pedhia tous fitites tous ilikiomenous
Are admission fees lower on any special day?	Υπάρχει ειδική μέρα με χαμηλότερη είσοδο;	Iparhi idhiki mera me hamiloteri issodho
Admission free	*Ελεύθερη είσοδος	Eleftheri issodhos
Have you got a ticket?	*Έχετε εισιτήριο;	Ehete issitirio
Where do I buy a ticket?	Που θ'αγοράσω ένα εισιτήριο;	Pou thaghorasso ena issitirio
Please leave your bag in the cloakroom	*Παρακαλώ αφήστε την τσάντα σας στη γκαρνταρόμπα	Parakalo afiste tin tsanda sas sti gardaroba
It's over there	*Είναι εκεί	Ine eki
Where is the … collection/exhibition?	Που είναι η συλλογή …/η έχθεση …;	Pou ine i siloghi/i ekthessi
Can I take photographs?	Επιτρέπεται να φωτογραφίσω;	Epitrepete na fotohrafisso
Can I use a tripod?	Επιτρέπεται να χρησιμοποιήσω τρίποδο;	Epitrepete na hrisimopiisso tripodho
Photographs are not allowed	*Δεν επιτρέπονται οι φωτογραφίες	Dhen epitreponde i fotohrafies

I want to buy a catalogue	Θέλω ν'αγοράσω έναν κατάλογο	Thelo naghorasso enan katalogho
Will you make photocopies?	Κάνετε φωτοαντίγραφα;	Kanete fotoandighrafa
Could you make me a transparency of this painting?	Μπορείτε να μου κάνετε μιά διαφάνεια αυτού του πίνακα;	Borite na mou kanete mia dhiafania aftou tou pinaka
How long will it take?	Πόσο θα πάρει;	Posso tha pari

HISTORICAL SITES

We want to visit ..., can we get there by car?	Θέλουμε να επισκεφτούμε ..., μπορούμε να πάμε με το αυτοκίνητο;	Theloume na episkeftoume ..., boroume na pame me to aftokinito
Is there far to walk?	Απέχει πολύ με τα πόδια;	Apehi poli me ta podhia
Is it an easy walk?	Είναι εύκολο να πάει κανείς με τα πόδια;	Ine efkolo na pai kanis me ta podhia
Is there access for wheelchairs?	Μπορούν να περάσουν αναπηρικά καροτσάκια;	Boroun na perasoun anapirika karotsakia
Is it far to the aqueduct? the castle? the fort? the fountain? the gate?	Απέχει πολύ το υδραγωγείο; το κάστρο; το φρούριο; η πηγή; η πύλη;	Apehi poli to idhraghoghio to kastro to frourio i pighi i pili

Is it far to the walls/fortifications?	Απέχουν πολύ τα τείχη/το οχυρό;	Apehoun poli ta tihi/to ohiro
When was it built?	Πότε κτίστηκε;	Pote ktistike
Who built it?	Ποιός το έκτισε;	Pios to ektisse
Where is the old part of the city?	Που είναι η παλιά πόλη;	Pou ine i palia poli
What is this building?	Τι είναι αυτό το κτίριο;	Ti ine afto to ktirio
Where is the house? church? cemetery?	Που είναι η οικία; η εκκλησία; το νεκροταφείο;	Pou ine i ikia i eklissia to nekrotafio

GARDENS, PARKS AND ZOOS

Where is the botanical garden/the zoo?	Που βρίσκεται ο βοτανικός κήπος/ο ζωολογικός κήπος;	Pou vriskete o votanikos kipos/o zoologhikos kipos
How do we get to the park?	Πως μπορούμε να πάμε στο πάρκο;	Pos boroume na pame sto parko
Can we walk there?	Μπορούμε να πάμε με τα πόδια;	Boroume na pame me ta podhia
Can we drive through the park?	Επιτρέπεται να πάμε με τ'αυτοκίνητο μέσα από το πάρκο;	Epitrepete na pame me taftokinito messapo to parko
Are the gardens open to the public?	Είναι ανοικτοί στο κοινό οι κήποι;	Ine anikti sto kino i kipi
What time do the gardens close?	Τι ώρα κλείνουν οι κήποι;	Ti ora klinoun i kipi

Is there a plan of the gardens?	Υπάρχει σχέδιο των κήπων;	Iparhi skhedhio ton kipon
Who designed the gardens?	Ποιός σχεδίασε τους κήπους;	Pios skhedhiasse tous kipous
Where is the tropical plant house?	Που είναι το θερμοκήπιο των τροπικών φυτών;	Pou ine to thermokipio ton tropikon fiton
Where is the lake?	Που είναι η λίμνη;	Pou ine i limni

EXPLORING

I'd like to walk around the old town	Θα ήθελα να τριγυρίσω την παλιά πόλη	Tha ithela na trighirisso tin palia poli
Is there a good street plan showing the buildings?	Υπάρχει κανένας καλός οδικός χάρτης που να δείχνει τα κτίρια;	Iparhi kanenas kalos odhikos hartis pou na dhihni ta ktiria
We want to visit	Θέλουμε να επισκεφτούμε	Theloume na episkeftoume
the cathedral	τη μητρόπολη	ti mitropoli
the fortress	το φρούριο	to frourio
the library	τη βιβλιοθήκη	ti vivliothiki
the monastery	το μοναστήρι	to monastiri
the palace	το παλάτι/το ανάκτορο	to palati/to anaktoro
the ruins	τα ερείπια	ta eripia
May we walk around the walls?	Μπορούμε να περπατήσουμε γύρω από τα τείχη;	Boroume na perpatissoume ghiro apo ta tihi

| May we go up the tower? | Μπορούμε να ανεβούμε στον πύργο; | Boroume na anevoume ston pirgho |
| Where is the antiques market/the flea market? | Που είναι η αγορά για αντίκες/τα παλιατζήδικα; | Pou ine i aghora ghia antikes/ta paliatzidhika |

GOING TO CHURCH

Is there a/an Catholic church?	Υπάρχει Καθολική εκκλησία;	Iparhi katholiki eklissia
Protestant church?	Προτεσταντική εκκλησία;	protestandiki eklissia
Orthodox church?	Ορθόδοξος Εκκλησία;	orthodoksos eklissia
Mosque?	Τζαμί;	tzami
Synagogue?	Συναγωγή;	sinaghoghi
What time is the service/mass?	Τι ώρα είναι η λειτουργία/ ακολουθία;	Ti ora ine i litourghia/ akolouthia
I'd like to look around the church	Θα ήθελα να ρίξω μιά ματιά γύρω στην εκκλησία	Tha ithela na rikso mia matia ghiro stin eklissia
When was the church built?	Πότε κτίστηκε η εκκλησία;	Pote ktistike i eklissia
Should women cover their head?	Πρέπει να καλύψουν οι γυναίκες το κεφάλι τους;	Prepi na kalipsoun i ghinekes to kefali tous

ENTERTAINMENT

Is there an entertainment guide?	Έχετε οδηγό ψυχαγωγικό;	Ehete odhigho psihaghoghiko
What's on at the theatre/cinema?	Τι παίζει στο θέατρο/στον κινηματόγραφο;	Ti pezi sto theatro/ston kinimatoghrafo
Is there a concert on this evening?	Έχει καμμιά συναυλία απόψε;	Ehi kamia sinavlia apopse
I want two seats for tonight/the matinée tomorrow	Θέλω δύο θέσεις γιά απόψε/γιά την απογευματινή παράσταση αύριο	Thelo dhio thessis ghia apopse/ghia tin apoghevmatini parastassi avrio
I want to book seats for Thursday	Θέλω να κλείσω θέσεις γιά την Πέμπτη	Thelo na klisso thessis ghia tin pempti
We're sold out (for that performance)	*Δεν έχουμε άλλα εισιτήρια (γι'αυτή την παράσταση)	Dhen ehoume ala issitiria (ghiafti tin parastassi)

Is the matinée sold out?	Δεν υπάρχουν εισιτήρια γιά την απογευματινή παράσταση;	Dhen iparhoun issitiria ghia tin apoghevmatini parastassi
I'd like seats in the stalls/for the circle	Θα ήθελα θέσεις στη πλατεία/στον εξώστης	Tha ithela thessis sti platia/ston eksostis
The cheapest seats please	Τις πιό φτηνές θέσεις παρακαλώ	Tis pio ftines thessis parakalo
Can you recommend	Μπορείτε να μου συστήσετε	Borite na mou sistissete
a good ballet?	ένα καλό μπαλλέτο;	ena kalo baleto
a good film?	ένα καλό φιλμ;	ena kalo film
a good musical?	μιά καλή μουσικοχορευτική παράσταση;	mia kali moussikohoreftiki parastassi
Who is directing/ conducting?	Ποιός είναι ο σκηνοθέτης/ μαέστρος;	Pios ine o skinothetis/ maestros
Who is singing?	Ποιός τραγουδάει;	Pios traghoudhai
Where are these seats?	Που είναι αυτές οι θέσεις;	Pou ine aftes i thessis
What time does the performance start?	Τι ώρα αρχίζει η παράσταση;	Ti ora arhizi i parastassi
What time does it end?	Τι ώρα τελειώνει;	Ti ora telioni
Is evening dress necessary?	Είναι αναγκαστικό το βραδινό φόρεμα;	Ine anangastiko to vradhino forema
Where is the cloakroom?	Που είναι το γκαρνταρόμπα;	Pou ine to gardaroba

This is your seat	*Αυτή είναι η θέσις σας	Afti ine i thessis sas
A programme, please	Ένα πρόγραμμα παρακαλώ	Ena proghrama parakalo
Where are the best nightclubs?	Που είναι τα καλύτερα νυχτερινά κέντρα;	Pou ine ta kalitera nikterina kentra
What time is the floor show?	Τι ώρα αρχίζει το παράσταση;	Ti ora arhizi to parastassi
Where can we go dancing?	Που να πάμε γιά να χορέψουμε;	Pou na pame ghia na horepsoume
Where is the best discotheque?	Που είναι το καλύτερο ντισκοτέκ;	Pou ine to kalitero discotheque
Would you like to dance?	Χορεύετε;	Horevete
May I have this dance?	Θέλετε να χορέψουμε;	Thelete na horepsoume
Is there a discotheque here?	Υπάρχει εδώ κανένα χορευτικό κέντρο/ ντισκοτέκ;	Iparhi edho kanena horeftikorr kentro/ discotheque
Can you recommend a good show?	Μπορείτε να μου συστήσετε καμμία καλή παράσταση;	Borite na mou sistissete kamia kali parastassi

SPORTS & GAMES

Where is the nearest tennis court/golf course?	Που είναι το πλησιέστερο γήπεδο τέννις/ γκόλφ;	Pou ine to plissiestero ghipedho tennis/golf
What is the charge per game? per hour? per day?	Πόσο κάνει το παιχνίδι; την ώρα; την μέρα;	Posso kani to pehnidhi tin ora tin mera
Is it a club?	Είναι κλόμπ;	Ine klob
Do I need temporary membership?	Πρέπει να γίνω προσωρινό μέλος;	Prepi na ghino prossorino melos
Where can we go swimming/fishing?	Που μπορούμε να κολυμπήσουμε/ ψαρέψουμε;	Pou boroume na kolimbissoume/ psarepsoume
Can I hire a racket? clubs? fishing tackle?	Μπορώ να νοικιάσω μια ρακέτα; κλόμπ; σύνεργα γιά ψάρεμα;	Boro na nikiasso mia raketa klob sinergha ghia psarema

Do I need a permit?	Χρειάζομαι άδεια;	Hriazome adhia
Where do I get a permit?	Που μπορώ να βγάλω άδεια;	Pou boro na vgalo adhia
Can we swim in the river?	Μπορούμε να κολυμπήσουμε στο ποτάμι;	Boroume na kolimbissoume sto potami
Is there an open air/ indoor swimming pool?	Υπάρχει ανοιχτή/ κλειστή πισίνα;	Iparhi anikti/klisti pissina
Is it heated?	Θερμαίνεται;	Thermenete
Is there a skating rink?	Υπάρχει πίστα παγοδρομίας;	Iparhi pista paghodhromias
Can I hire skates/ skiing equipment?	Μπορώ να νοικιάσω παγοπέδιλα/ εξοπλισμό γιά σκι;	Boro na nikiasso paghopedhila/exoplismo ghia ski
Can I take lessons here?	Μπορώ να κάνω μαθήματα εδώ;	Boro na kano mathimata edho
I've never skied before	Δεν έχω ξανακάνει σκι	Dhen eho ksanakani ski
Are there ski runs for beginners/average skiers?	Υπάρχουν χιονόδρομοι σκι γιά αρχάριους/ προχωρηημένους;	Iparhoun hionodhromi ski ghi arharious/ prohorimenous
Are there ski lifts?	Υπάρχουν ανελκυστήρες σκι;	Iparhoun anelkistires ski
We want to go to a football match/to the tennis tournament	Θέλουμε να πάμε σ'ένα ποδοσφαιρικό αγώνα/στο τουρνουά τέννις	Theloume na pame sena podhosferiko aghona/ sto tournoua tennis

Can you get us tickets?	Μπορείτε να μας βγάλετε εισιτήρια;	Borite na mas vgalete issitiria
Are there any seats in the grandstand?	Υπάρχουν θέσεις στη μεγάλη εξέδρα;	Iparhoun thessis sti meghali exedhra
How much are the cheapest seats?	Πόσο κάνουν οι πιό φτηνές θέσεις;	Posso kanoun i pio ftines thessis
Are they in the sun or the shade?	Είναι στον ήλιο η στη σκιά;	Ine ston ilio i sti skia
Who is playing?	Ποιός παίζει;	Pios pezi
When does it start?	Τι ώρα αρχίζει;	Ti ora arhizi
Who is winning?	Ποιός κερδίζει;	Pios kerdhizi
What is the score?	Ποιό είναι το αποτέλεσμα;	Pio ine to apotelesma
I'd like to ride	Θα ήθελα να κάνω ιππασία	Tha ithela na kano ipassia
Is there a riding stable nearby?	Υπάρχει σταύλος γιά ιππασία εδώ κοντά;	Iparhi stavlos ghia ipassia edho konda
Do you give lessons?	Κάνετε μαθήματα;	Kanete mathimata
I am an inexperienced/a good rider	Είμαι άπειρος/καλός ιππεύς	Ime apiros/kalos ipefs
Where is the racecourse?	Που είναι ο ιππόδρομος;	Pou ine o ipodhromos
Which is the favourite?	Ποιό είναι το φαβορί;	Pio ine to favori
Who is the jockey?	Ποιός είναι ο τζόκευ;	Pios ine o jockey
... (amount) to win on ...	... γιά νίκη στο ...	Ghia niki sto

... (amount) for a place	... γιά θέση	... ghia thessi
What are the odds?	Ποιές είναι οι πιθανότητες;	Pies ine i pithanotites
I'd like to try waterskiing	Θα ήθελα να δοκιμάσω θαλάσσιο σκι	Tha ithela na dhokimasso thalassio ski
I haven't waterskied before	Δεν έχω κάνει θαλάσσιο σκι ποτέ	Dhen eho kani thalassio ski pote
Can I rent/borrow a wetsuit?	Μπορώ να νοικιάσω/δανειστώ μιά αδιάβροχη φόρμα;	Boro na nikiasso/dhanisto mia adhiavrohi forma
Should I wear a life jacket?	Πρέπει να φορέσω σωσίβιο;	Prepi na foresso sossivio
Can I hire a rowing boat? a motor boat? a surfboard?	Μπορώ να νοικιάσω βάρκα με κουπιά; βάρκα με μηχανή; σανίδα κολυμπίσεως;	Boro na nikiasso varka me koupia varka me mihani sanida kolimbiseos
Is there a map of the river?	Υπάρχει χάρτης του ποταμού;	Iparhi hartis tou potamou
Can we buy fuel here?	Μπορούμε να αγοράσουμε καύσιμα εδώ;	Boroume naghorassoume kafsima edho

ON THE BEACH[1]

Where are the best beaches?	Που είναι οι καλύτερες πλαζ;	Pou ine i kaliteres plaz
Is there a quiet beach near here?	Υπάρχει καμμιά ήσυχη παραλία εδώ κοντά;	Iparhi kamia issihi paralia edho konta
Can we walk or is it too far?	Μπορούμε να πάμε με τα πόδια η είναι πολύ μακρυά;	Boroume na pame me ta podhia i ine poli makria
Is there a bus to the beach?	Έχει λεωφορείο γιά την πλαζ;	Ehi leoforio ghia tin plaz
Is the beach sandy or rocky?	Είναι η παραλία με βράχεια η με άμμο;	Ine i paralia me vrahia i me amo
Is it safe for small children?	Είναι ασφαλές γιά μικρά παιδιά;	Ine asfales ghia mikra pedhia

1. See also SPORTS & GAMES, p. 157.

Is the sea rough here?	Είναι άγρια η θάλασσα εδώ;	Ine aghria i thalassa edho
Is it dangerous to bathe here?	Είναι επικίνδυνο να κολυμπήση κανείς εδώ;	Ine epikindhino na kolimbissi kanis edho
Is it safe for swimming?	Είναι ασφαλές γιά κολύμπι;	Ine asfales ghia kolimbi
Is there a lifeguard?	Υπάρχει ναυαγοσώστης;	Iparhi navaghossostis
What time is high tide?	Τι ώρα έχει ρουσκονεριά;	Ti ora ehi rouskhoneria
Bathing prohibited	*Απαγορεύεται η κολύμβηση	Apaghorevete i kolimvissi
Diving prohibited	*Απαγορεύονται οι βουτιές	Apaghorevonte i vouties
It's dangerous	*Είναι επικίνδυνο	Ine epikindhino
There's a strong current here	*Έχει πολύ δυνατό ρεύμα εδώ	Ehi poli dhinato revma edho
Are you a strong swimmer?	*Είσαι καλός κολυμβητής;	Isse kalos kolimvitis
Is it deep?	Είναι βαθύ;	Ine vathi
How's the water?	Πως είναι το νερό;	Pos ine to nero
It's warm/cold	Είναι ζεστό/κρύο	Ine zesto/krio
Can one swim in the lake?	Μπορεί κανείς να κολυμπήση στη λίμνη;	Bori kanis na kolimbissi sti limni
Is there an indoor/ outdoor swimming pool?	Υπάρχει κλειστή/ ανοικτή πισίνα;	Iparhi klisti/anikti pissina

Is it salt or fresh water?	Είναι με θαλασσινό η με γλυκό νερό;	Ine me thalassino i me ghliko nero
Are there showers?	Υπάρχουν ντους;	Iparhoun douz
I want a cabin for the day for the morning for two hours	Θέλω μία καμπίνα γιά όλη τη μέρα γιά το πρωί γιά δύο ώρες	Thelo mia cabina ghia oli ti mera ghia to proi ghia dhio ores
I want to hire a deckchair/sunshade	Θέλω να νοικιάσω μιά σεζλόγκ/ ομπρέλλα	Thelo na nikiasso mia chaiz long/ombrella
Where's the harbour?	Που είναι το λιμάνι;	Pou ine to limani
Can we go out in a fishing boat?	Μπορούμε να πάμε με βάρκα;	Boroume na pame me varka
We want to go fishing	Θέλουμε να πάμε γιά ψάρεμα	Theloume na pame ghia psarema
Is there any underwater fishing?	Έχει καθόλου υποβρύχειο ψάρεμα;	Ehi katholou ipovrihio psarema
Can I hire a boat?	Μπορώ να νοικιάσω μιά βάρκα;	Boro na nikiasso mia varka
What does it cost by the hour?	Πόσο κάνει την ώρα;	Posso kani tin ora

IN THE COUNTRY

Is there a scenic route to …?	Υπάρχει γραφική διαδρομή γιά το …;	Iparhi ghrafiki dhiadhromi ghia to
Can you give me a lift to …?	Μπορείτε να με πάτε ώς το …;	Borite na me pate os to
Is there a footpath to …?	Υπάρχει μονοπάτι γιά το …;	Iparhi monopati ghia to
Is it possible to go across country?	Μπορεί κανείς να πάει περπατώντας μέσα από τους αγρούς;	Bori kanis na pai perpatondas mesa apo tous aghrous
Is there a shortcut?	Μπορεί κανείς να κόψει δρόμο;	Bori kanis na kopsi dhromo
Is this a public footpath?	Είναι αυτό δημόσιο μονοπάτι;	Ine afto dhimossio monopati
Is there a bridge across the stream?	Έχει γέφυρα που να περνάει το ποτάμι;	Ehi ghefira pou na pernai to potami

Can we walk?	Μπορούμε να περπατήσουμε;	Boroume na perpatissoume
How far is the next village?	Πόσο απέχει το επόμενο χωριό;	Posso apehi to epomeno horio
What do you call these flowers? birds? trees?	Πως τα λένε αυτά τα λουλούδια; πουλιά; δέντρα;	Pos ta lene afta ta louloudhia poulia dhendra

TRAVELLING
WITH CHILDREN

Can you put a child's bed/cot in our room?	Μπορείτε να βάλετε ένα παιδικό κρεββατάκι/κούνια στο δωμάτιο μας;	Borite na valete ena pedhiko krevataki/ kounia sto dhomatio mas
Can you give us adjoining rooms?	Μπορείτε να μας δώσετε δωμάτια που να επικοινωνούν;	Borite na mas dhossete dhomatia pou na epikinonoun
Does the hotel have a baby-sitter service?	Έχει το ξενοδοχείο υπηρεσία γιά μπέϊμπισιτερ;	Ehi to ksenodhohio ipiressia ghia baby-sitter
Can you find me a baby-sitter?	Μπορείτε να μου βρείτε μπέϊμπισιτερ;	Borite na mou vrite baby-sitter
We shall be out for a couple of hours	Θα βγούμε έξω γιά περίπου δύο ώρες	Tha vghoume ekso ghia peripou dhio ores
We shall be back at ...	Θα γυρίσουμε στις ...	Tha ghirissoume stis

Is there a children's menu?	Έχετε μενού γιά παιδιά;	Ehete menou ghia pedhia
Do you have (half) portions for children?	Έχετε παιδικές (μισές) μερίδες;	Ehete pedhikes (mises) meridhes
Have you got a high chair?	Έχετε παιδική καρέκλα;	Ehete pedhiki karekla
Are there any organized activities for children?	Υπάρχουν παιδικές δραστηριότητες;	Iparhoun pedhikes dhrastiriotites
Is there a	Έχετε	Ehete
children's swimming pool?	πισίνα γιά παιδιά;	pissina ghia pedhia
playground?	παιδική χαρά;	pedhiki hara
games room?	αίθουσα με παιχνίδια;	ethoussa me pehnidhia
Is there	Υπάρχει	Iparhi
an amusement park	λουναπάρκ	lounapark
a zoo	ζωολογικός κήπος	zoöloghikos kipos
a toyshop	κατάστημα παιχνιδιών	katastima pehnidhion
nearby?	εδώ κοντά;	edho konda
I'd like	Θέλω	Thelo
a beach ball	μιά μπάλλα γιά την παραλία	mia bala ghia tin paralia
a bucket and spade	ένας κουβαδάκι και ένα φτυάρι	enas kouvadhaki ke ena ftiari
a doll	μία κούκλα	mia koukla
some flippers	βατραχοπέδιλα	vatrahopedhila
some goggles	μάσκα γιά θάλασσα	maska ghia thalassa
some playing cards	χαρτιά	hartia
some roller skates	πατίνια με ρόδες	patinia me rhodes

a snorkel	αναπνευστήρας	anapnevstiras
Where can I feed/ change my baby?	Που μπορώ να ταΐσω/ν'αλλάξω το μωρό;	Pou boro na taiso/nalakso to moro
Can you heat this bottle for me?	Μπορείτε να μου ζεστάνετε αυτό το μπουκάλι;	Borite na mou zestanete afto to boukali
I want some disposable nappies	Θέλω πάνες γιά βρέφη γιά μιά μόνο χρήση	Thelo panes ghia vrefi ghia mia mono hrissi
a feeding bottle some baby food	ένα μπιμπερό παιδικές τροφές	ena bibero pedhikes trofes
My daughter suffers from travel sickness	Η κόρη μου υποφέρει από ναυτία	I kori mou ipoferi apo naftia
He/she has hurt himself/herself	Έχει πληγωθεί	Ehi plighothi
My son is ill	Ο γιός μου είναι άρρωστος	O ghios mou ine arostos
He has lost his toy	Έχασε το παιχνίδι του	Ehasse to peghnidhi tou
I'm sorry if they have bothered you	Με συγχωρείτε αν σας ενόχλησαν	Me sinhorite an sas enohlissan

BUSINESS MATTERS[1]

I would like to make an appointment with ...	Θα ήθελα να κλείσω ένα ραντεβού με ...	Tha ithela na klisso ena rendezvous me
I have an appointment with ...	Έχω ένα ραντεβού με ...	Eho ena rendezvous me
My name is ...	Το όνομα μου είναι ...	To onoma mou ine
Here is my card	Να η κάρτα μου	Na i karta mou
This is our catalogue	Αυτός είναι ο κατάλογος μας	Aftos ine o kataloghos mas
I would like to see your products	Θα ήθελα να δω τα προϊόντα σας	Tha ithela na dho ta proïonda sas
Could you send me some samples?	Μπορείτε να μου στείλετε μερικά δείγματα;	Borite na mou stilete merika dhigmata

1. See also TELEPHONING (p. 143).

| Can you provide an interpreter/a secretary? | Μπορείτε να μου δώσετε ένα διερμηνέα/μία γραμματέα; | Borite na mou dhossete ena dhierminea/mia ghramatea |
| Where can I make some photocopies? | Που μπορώ να κάνω μερικά φωτοαντίγραφα; | Pou boro na kano merika fotoandighrafa |

AT THE DOCTOR'S

AILMENTS

I must see a doctor; can you recommend one?	Πρέπει να δω ένα γιατρό. Μπορείτε να μου συστήσετε έναν;	Prepi na dho ena ghiatro. Borite na mou sistissete enan
Is there a doctor's surgery near here?	Υπάρχει κανένα ιατρείο εδώ κοντά;	Iparhi kanena iatrio edho konta
Please call a doctor	Φωνάξτε σας παρακαλώ ένα γιατρό	Fonakste sas parakalo ena ghiatro
When can the doctor come?	Πότε μπορεί να έρθει ο γιατρός;	Pote bori na erthi o ghiatros
Does the doctor speak English?	Μιλάει αγγλικά ο γιατρός;	Milai anglika o ghiatros

Can I make an appointment for as soon as possible?	Μπορώ να κλείσω ένα ραντεβού όσο γίνεται πιό σύντομα	Boro na klisso ena rendezvous osso ghinete pio sintoma
I take ..., can you give me a prescription please	Παίρνω ... μου δίνετε συνταγή παρακαλώ	Perno ... mou dhinete sintaghi parakalo
I have high/low blood pressure	Έχω υψηλή/χαμηλή πίεση	Eho ipsili/hamili piessi
I am pregnant	Είμαι έγκυος	Ime engios
I am allergic to ...	Είμαι αλλεργικός η ...	Ime alerghikos i
I think it is infected	Νομίζω ότι έχε μολυνθεί	Nomizo oti ehi molinthi
I am ill	Είμαι άρρωστος	Ime arostos
I have a fever	Έχω πυρετό	Eho pireto
I've a pain in my right arm	Μου πονάει το δεξί μου χέρι	Mou ponai to dheksi mou heri
My wrist hurts	Μου πονάει ο καρπός του χεριού μού	Mou ponai o karpos tou heriou mou
I think I've sprained/ broken my ankle	Νομίζω ότι έχω στραμπουλήξει/ σπάσει τον αστράγαλο μου	Nomizo oti eho strambouliksi/spassi ton astraghalo mou
I fell down and hurt my back	Έπεσα και κτύπησα τη πλάτη μου	Epessa ke ktipissa ti plati mou
My feet are swollen	Τα πόδια μου είναι πρισμένα	Ta podhia mou ine prismena

I've burned/cut/ bruised myself	**Κάηκα/κόπηκα/ μωλωπίστηκα**	Kaika/kopika/molopistika
My stomach is upset	**Το στομάχι μου είναι χαλασμένο**	To stomahi mou ine halasmeno
My appetite's gone	**Δεν έχω όρεξη**	Dhen eho oreksi
I think I've got food poisoning	**Νομίζω πώς έπαθα τροφική δηλητηρίαση**	Nomizo pos epatha trofiki dhilitiriassi
I can't eat/sleep	**Δεν μπορώ να φάω/ να κοιμηθώ**	Dhen boro na fao/na kimitho
My nose keeps bleeding	**Η μύτη μου ανοίγει συνεχώς**	I miti mou anighi sinehos
I have earache	**Μου πονάν τ'αυτιά μου**	Mou ponan taftia mou
I have difficulty in breathing	**Αναπνέω με δυσκολία**	Anapneo me dhiskolia
I feel dizzy/sick/ shivery	**Αισθάνομαι ζάλη/ ναυτία/ρίγος**	Esthanome zali/naftia /righos
I keep vomiting	**Κάνω συνεχώς εμετό**	Kano sinehos emeto
I have a temperature	**Έχω πυρετό**	Eho pireto
I think I've caught 'flu	**Νομίζω πώς έπαθα γρίππη**	Nomizo pos epatha ghripi
I've got a cold	**Κρυολόγησα**	Kriologhissa
I've had it since yesterday	**Το έχω από χθες**	To eho apo hthes
I've had it for a few hours	**Το έχω μερικές ώρες τώρα**	To eho merikes ores tora
abscess	**απόστημα**	apostima
ache	**πόνος**	ponos

allergy	αλλεργία	alerghia
appendicitis	σκωληκοειδίτις	skolikoidhitis
arthritis	αρθρίτις	arthritis
asthma	άσθμα	asthma
back pain	πόνος πλάτης	ponos platis
blister	φουσκάλα	fouskala
boil	καλόγερος	kalogheros
bruise	μελανιά	melania
burn	κάψιμο/έγκαυμα	kapsimo/engavma
cardiac condition	καρδιακή πάθησις	kardhiaki pathissis
chill, cold	κρύωμα	krioma
constipation	δυσκοιλιότητα	dhiskiliotita
cough	βήχας	vihas
cramp	κράμπα	kramba
diabetes	διαβήτης	dhiavitis
diarrhoea	διάρροια	dhiaria
earache	πόνος αυτιών	ponos aftion
fever	πυρετός	piretos
food poisoning	τροφική δηλητηρίασις	trofiki dhilitiriassis
fracture	σπάσιμο	spassimo
hay fever	αλλεργία	alerghia
headache	πονοκέφαλος	ponokefalos
high blood pressure	υψηλή πίεση	ipsili piessi
ill, sick	άρρωστος	arostos
illness	αρρώστια	arostia

indigestion	δυσπεψία	dhispepsia
infection	μόλυνσις	molinsis
influenza	γρίππη	ghripi
insect bite	τσίμπημα εντόμου	tsimbima endomou
insomnia	άϋπνία	aipnia
itch	φαγούρα	faghoura
nausea	ναυτία	naftia
nose bleed	μάτωμα μύτης	matoma mitis
pain	πόνος	ponos
rheumatism	ρευματισμός	revmatismos
sore throat	ερεθισμένος λαιμός/ πονόλαιμος	erethismenos lemos/ ponolemos
sprain	στραγγούλισμα	strangoulisma
sting	τσίμπημα	tsimbima
stomache-ache	πόνος στομαχιού	ponos stomahiou
sunburn	ηλιόκαμα	iliokama
sunstroke	ηλίαση	iliassi
swelling	πρήξιμο	priksimo
tonsillitis	αμυγδαλίτις	amighdhalitis
toothache	πονόδοντας	ponodhondas
ulcer	έλκος	elkos
wound	πληγή	plighi

TREATMENT

Do you have a temperature?	*Έχετε πυρετό;	Ehete pireto
Where does it hurt?	*Που πονάει;	Pou ponai
Have you a pain here?	*Πονάτε εδώ;	Ponate edho
How long have you had the pain/been suffering from …?	*Από πότε αρχίσατε να πονάτε/να υποφέρετε από …;	Apo pote arhissate na ponate/na ipoferete apo …
Open your mouth	*Ανοίξτε το στόμα σας	Anikste to stoma sas
Put out your tongue	*Βγάλτε τη γλῶσσα σας	Vghalte ti ghlossa sas
Breathe in	*Εισπνεύστε	Ispnefste
Hold your breath	*Κρατήστε την αναπνοή σας	Kratiste tin anapnoi sas
Does that hurt?	*Πονάει;	Ponai
A lot or a little?	*Πολύ ή λίγο;	Poli i ligho
Lie down	*Ξαπλώστε	Ksaploste
I will need a specimen	*Θα χρειαστώ ένα δείγμα	Tha hriasto ena dhighma
What medicine have you been taking?	*Τι φάρμακα παίρνετε;	Ti farmaka pernete
Take these pills/this medicine	*Πάρτε αυτά τα χάπια/αυτό το φάρμακο	Parte afta ta hapia/afto to farmako
I will give you an antibiotic/sedative	*Θα σας δώσω αντιβιοτικό/καταπραϋντικό	Tha sas dhosso antiviotiko/katapraintiko

Take this prescription to the chemist's	*Πάρτε αυτή τη συνταγή στο φαρμακείο	Parte afti ti sintaghi sto farmakio
Take this three times a day	*Πάρτε το τρεις φορές τη μέρα	Parte to tris fores ti mera
I'll give you an injection	*Θα σας κάνω μία ένεση	Tha sas kano mia enessi
Roll up your sleeve	*Ανεβάστε το μανίκι σας	Anevaste to maniki sas
You should stay on a diet for a few days	*Πρέπει να κάνετε δίαιτα γιά λίγες μέρες	Prepi na kanete dhieta ghia lighes meres
Come and see me again in two days' time	*Ελάτε να με ξαναδείτε σε δύο μέρες	Elate na mè ksanadhite se dhio meres
Your leg must be X-rayed	*Πρέπει να γίνη μιά ακτινογραφία του ποδιού σας	Prepi na ghini mia aktinoghrafia tou podhiou sas
You must go to hospital	*Πρέπει να πάτε στο νοσοκομείο	Prepi na pate sto nossokomio
I feel better now	Αισθάνομαι καλύτερα τώρα	Esthanome kalitera tora
How much do I owe you?	Τι σας ωφείλω;	Ti sas ofilo
I'd like a receipt for the health insurance	Θα ήθελα μιά απόδειξη γιά την ασφάλεια υγείας	Tha ithela mia apodhiksi ghia tin asfalia ighias
You should not travel until ...	*Δεν πρέπει να ταξιδέψετε μέχρι ...	Dhen prepi na taksidhepsete mehri

Nothing to worry about	*Δεν υπάρχει λόγος ν'ανησυχήτε	Dhen iparhi loghos nanissihite
You're hurting me	Πονάω	Ponao
Must I stay in bed?	Πρέπει να μείνω στο κρεβάτι;	Prepi na mino sto krevati
Will you come and see me again?	Θα'ρθετε να με ξαναδείτε;	Tharthete na me ksanadhite
When do you think I can leave?	Πότε μπορώ να φύγω;	Pote boro na figho
ambulance	νοσοκομειακό αυτοκίνητο	nossokomiako aftokinito
anaesthetic	αναισθητικό	anesthitiko
aspirin	ασπιρίνη	aspirini
bandage	επίδεσμος	epidhesmos
chiropodist	ποδίατρος	podhiatros
hospital	νοσοκομείο	nossokomio
injection	ένεση	enessi
laxative	καθαρκτικό	katharktiko
nurse	νοσοκόμα	nossokoma
operation	εγχείρηση	enhirissi
optician	οφθαλμίατρος	ofthalmiatros
osteopath	χειροπράκτωρ	hiropraktor
pill	χάπι	hapi
(adhesive) plaster	λευκοπλάστης	lefkoplastis
prescription	συνταγή	sintaghi
X-ray	ακτινογραφία	aktinoghrafia

PARTS OF THE BODY

ankle	**αστράγαλος**	astraghalos
arm	**μπράτσο**	bratso
back	**πλάτη**	plati
bladder	**κύστις**	kistis
blood	**αίμα**	ema
body	**σώμα**	soma
bone	**κόκκαλο**	kokalo
bowels	**έντερα**	endera
brain	**μυαλό**	mialo
breast	**στήθος**	stithos
cheek	**μάγουλο**	maghoulo
chest	**στήθος**	stithos
chin	**πηγούνι**	pighouni
collar-bone	**κλειδοκόκκαλο**	klidhokokalo
ear	**αυτί**	afti
elbow	**αγγώνας**	angonas
eye	**μάτι**	mati
eyelid	**βλέφαρο**	vlefaro
face	**πρόσωπο**	prossopo
finger	**δάκτυλο**	dhaktilo
foot	**πόδι**	podhi
forehead	**μέτωπο**	metopo
gum	**ούλο**	oulo

hand	χέρι	heri
head	κεφάλι	kefali
heart	καρδιά	kardhia
heel	φτέρνα	fterna
hip	ισχίον	iskhion
jaw	μασέλα	massela
joint	κλείδωσις	klidhossis
kidney	νεφρό	nefro
knee	γόνατο	ghonato
knee-cap	επιγονατίς	epighonatis
leg	πόδι	podhi
lip	χείλος	hilos
liver	συκώτι	sikoti
lung	πνεύμονας	pnevmonas
mouth	στόμα	stoma
muscle	μύς	mis
nail	νύχι	nihi
neck	λαιμός	lemos
nerve	νεύρο	nevro
nose	μύτη	miti
rib	πλευρό	plevro
shoulder	ώμος	omos
skin	δέρμα	dherma
spine	σπονδυλική στήλη	spondhiliki stili
stomach	στομάχι	stomahi
temple	κρόταφος	krotafos

thigh	μηρός	miros
throat	λαιμός	lemos
thumb	αντίχειρ	antihir
toe	δάκτυλο ποδιού	dhaktilo podhiou
tongue	γλώσσα	ghlossa
tonsils	αμυγδαλές	amighdhales
tooth	δόντι	dhonti
vein	φλέβα	fleva
wrist	καρπός χεριού	karpos heriou

AT THE DENTIST'S

I must see a dentist	Πρέπει να δω έναν οδοντογιατρό	Prepi na dho enan odhontoghiatro
As soon as possible	Μπορώ να κλείσω ένα ραντεβού με τον οδοντογιατρό;	Boro na klisso ena rendezvous me ton odhontoghiatro
As soon as possible	Όσο το δυνατόν συντομώτερα	Osso to dhinaton sintomotera
I have toothache	Έχω πονόδοντο	Eho ponodhonto
This tooth hurts	Μου πονάει αυτό το δόντι	Mou ponai afto to dhonti
I've lost a filling	Μου έφυγε ένα βούλωμα	Mou efighe ena vouloma
I have a broken tooth	Έχω ένα σπασμένο δόντι	Eho ene spasmeno dhondi
Can you fill it?	Μπορείτε να μου το βουλώσετε;	Borite na mou to voulossete
Can you do it now?	Μπορείτε να το κάνετε τώρα;	Borite na to kanete tora

I do not want the tooth taken out	Δεν θέλω να βγει το δόντι	Dhen thelo na vgi to dhonti
Please give me an anaesthetic	Παρακαλώ δώστε μου αναισθητικό	Parakalo dhoste mou anesthitiko
My gums are swollen/ keep bleeding	Τα ούλα μου είναι πρισμένα/ ματώνουν	Ta oula mou ine prismena/matonoun
I have broken/chipped my dentures	Έσπασαν/ράγισαν οι μασέλες μου	Espassan/raghissan i masseles mou
Can you fix it (temporarily)?	Μπορείτε να το διορθώσετε (προσωρινά);	Borite na to dhiorthossete (prossorina)
You're hurting me	Με πονάτε	Me ponate
How much do I owe you?	Τι σας ωφείλω;	Ti sas ofilo
When should I come again?	Πότε να ξανάρθω;	Pote na ksanartho
Please rinse your mouth	*Παρακαλώ ξεπλύντε το στόμα σας	Parakalo kseplinte to stoma sas
I will X-ray your teeth	*Θα σας κάνω μία ακτινογραφία των δοντιών σας	Tha sas kano mia aktinoghrafia ton dhontion sas
You have an abscess	*Έχετε ένα απόστημα	Ehete ena apostima
The nerve is exposed	*Το νεύρο είναι εκτεθειμένο	To nevro ine ektethimeno
This tooth will have to come out	*Αυτό το δόντι πρέπει να βγεί	Afto to dhonti prepi na vgi

PROBLEMS & ACCIDENTS

There's a fire	Έχει πιάσει φωτιά	Ehi piasi fotia
It's urgent	Είναι επείγον	Ine epighon
Where's the police station?	Που είναι η αστυνομία;	Pou ine i astinomia
Call the police	Φωνάξτε την αστυνομία	Fonakste tin astinomia
Where is the British/American consulate?	Που είναι το Αγγλικό/Αμερικανικό Προξενείο;	Pou ine to angliko/amerikaniko proksenio
Please let the consulate know	Σας παρακαλώ ειδοποιείστε το Προξενείο	Sas parakalo idhopiiste to proksenio
My son/daughter is lost	Χάθηκε ο γιός μου/η κόρη μου	Hathike o ghios mou/i kori mou
My bag/wallet has been stolen	Η τσάντα/το πορτοφόλι μου εκλάπησσαν	I tsanta/to portofoli mou eklapissan

I found this in the street	Το βρήκα στο δρόμο	To vrika sto dhromo
I have lost my luggage/passport/ travellers' cheques	Έχασα τις αποσκευές/τό διαβατήριο/τά τράβελλερς τσέκς μου	Ehassa tis aposkeves/to dhiavatirio/ta travellers' cheques mou
Our car has been broken into	Το αυτοκίνητο μας έχει παραβιαστεί	To aftokinito mas ehi paraviasti
I've been robbed/ mugged	Μ'έκλεψαν	M'eklepsan
I have missed my train	Έχασα το τραίνο μου	Ehassa to treno mou
My luggage is on board	Οι αποσκευές μου έχουν επιβιβαστεί	I aposkeves mou ehoun epivivasthi
Call a doctor	Φωνάξτε ένα γιατρό	Fonakste ena ghiatro
Call an ambulance	Φωνάξτε ένα νοσοκομειακό αυτοκίνητο	Fonakste ena nossokomiako aftokinito
There has been an accident	Συνέβη ένα ατύχημα	Sinevi ena atihima
He's badly hurt	Είναι σοβαρά τραυματισμένος	Ine sovara travmatismenos
He has fainted	Λιποθύμησε	Lipothimisse
He's losing blood	Αιμορραγεί	Emoraghi
Her arm is broken	Έχει σπάσει το χέρι της	Ehi spassi to heri tis
Please get some water a blanket some bandages	Σας παρακαλώ φέρτε λίγο νερό μία κουβέρτα επιδέσμους	Sas parakalo ferte ligho nero mia kouverta epidhesmous

I've broken my glasses	Έσπασα τα γυαλιά μου	Espassa ta ghialia mou
I can't see	Δεν βλέπω	Dhen vlepo
A child has fallen in the water	Ένα παιδάκι έπεσε μέσ'στο νερό	Ena pedhaki epesse mesto nero
May I see your insurance certificate/driving licence?	*Μπορώ να δω το πιστοποιητικό ασφαλείας σας/ άδεια οδηγήσεως;	Boro na dho to pistopiitiko asfalias sas/adhia odhighisseos
Apply to the insurance company	*Ρωτήστε την ασφάλεια	Rotiste tin asfalia
What are the name and address of the owner?	Ποιό είναι το όνομα και την διεύθυνση του ιδιοκτήτη;	Pio ine to onoma ke tin dhiefthinsi tou idhioktiti
Are you willing to act as a witness?	Δέχεσται να έρθετε ως μάρτυς;	Dheheste na erthete os martis
I didn't understand the sign	Δεν κατάλαβα την πινακίδα	Dhen katalava tin pinakidha
How much is the fine?	Πόσο κάνει το πρόστιμο;	Posso kani to prostimo
Can I have your name and address, please?	Μπορώ να έχω το όνομα και την διεύθυνση σας, παρακαλώ;	Boro na eho to onoma ke tin dhiethinssi sas parakalo
Can you help me?	Μπορείτε να με βοηθήσετε;	Borite na me voithissete
I want a copy of the police report	Θέλω ένα αντίγραφο της αστυνομικής αναφοράς	Thelo ena antighrafo tis astinomikis anaforas

TIME & DATES

TIME

What time is it?[1]	**Τι ώρα είναι;**	Ti ora ine
It's one o'clock	**Είναι μία η ώρα**	Ine mia i ora
2 o'clock	**δύο η ώρα**	dhio i ora
quarter to ten	**δέκα παρά τέταρτο**	dheka para tetarto
quarter past five	**πέντε και τέταρτο**	pente ke tetarto
half past four	**τέσσερεις και μισή**	tesseris ke missi
five past eight	**οκτώ και πέντε**	okto ke pente
twenty to three	**τρεις παρά είκοσι**	tris para ikossi
Second	**Δευτερόλεπτο**	Dhefterolepto
Minute	**Λεπτό**	Lepto

1. To tell the time in Greek, if it is past the hour you will tell the hour and then the minutes (or quarters, half hour etc.) e.g. **dhodheka ke ikoss** = twelve twenty. After the half hour you tell the next hour *less* the minutes, e.g. **dhodheka para ikossi** = twenty minutes to twelve.

Hour	Ώρα	Ora
It's early/late	Είναι νωρίς/αργά	Ine noris/argha
My watch is slow/ fast/has stopped	Το ρολόι μου πάει σιγά/γρήγορα/ σταμάτησε	To roloi mou pai sigha/ ghrighora/stamatisse
Sorry I'm late	Συγγνώμη, άργησα	Sighnomi arghissa

DATE

What's the date?	Πόσες έχει ο μήνας;	Posses ehi o minas
It's 9 December	Είναι εννιά Δεκεμβρίου	Ine enia dhekemvriou
We're leaving on 5 January	Φεύγουμε στις πέντε Ιανουαρίου	Fevghoume stis pente ianouariou
We got here on 27 July	Φτάσαμε εδώ στις εικοσιεπτά Ιουλίου	Ftassame edho stis ikossiepta iouliou

DAY

Morning
  this morning
  in the morning
	Πρωί
	σήμερα το πρωί
	το πρωί
		Proi
		  simera to proi
		  to proi

Midday, noon	Μεσημέρι	Messimeri

Afternoon
  yesterday afternoon
	Απόγευμα
	χθες το απόγευμα
		Apoghevma
		  hthes to apoghevma

Evening
  tomorrow evening
	βράδυ
	αύριο το βράδυ
		vradhi
		  avrio to vradhi

Midnight	Μεσάνυχτα	Messanikta
Night	Νύκτα	Nikta
tonight	απόψε	apopse
last night	χθες το βράδυ	hthes to vradhi
Sunrise	Ανατολή	Anatoli
Dawn	Ξημέρωμα	Ksimeroma
Sunset	Δύση	Dhissi
Dusk, twilight	Σούρουπο	Souroupo
Today	Σήμερα	Simera
Yesterday	Χθες	Hthes
two days ago	προχθές	prohthes
Tomorrow	Αύριο	Avrio
in two days	μεθαύριο	methavrio
in ten days' time	σε δέκα μέρες	se dheka meres

WEEK

Sunday	Κυριακή	Kiriaki
Monday	Δευτέρα	Dheftera
Tuesday	Τρίτη	Triti
Wednesday	Τετάρτη	Tetarti
Thursday	Πέμπτη	Pempti
Friday	Παρασκευή	Paraskevi
Saturday	Σάββατο	Savato
On Tuesday	Την Τρίτη	Tin triti
On Sundays	Τις Κυριακές	Tis kiriakes
Fortnight	Δύο εβδομάδες	Dhio evdhomadhes

MONTH

January	**Ιανουάριος**	Ianouarios
February	**Φεβρουάριος**	Fevrouarios
March	**Μάρτιος**	Martios
April	**Απρίλιος**	Aprilios
May	**Μάϊος**	Maios
June	**Ιούνιος**	Iounios
July	**Ιούλιος**	Ioulios
August	**Αύγουστος**	Avghoustos
September	**Σεπτέμβριος**	Septemvrios
October	**Οκτώβριος**	Oktovrios
November	**Νοέμβριος**	Noemvrios
December	**Δεκέμβριος**	Dhekemvrios
In March	**Τον Μάρτιο**	Ton martio

SEASON

Spring	**Άνοιξη**	Aniksi
Summer	**Καλοκαίρι**	Kalokeri
Autumn, fall	**Φθινόπωρο**	Fthinoporo
Winter	**Χειμώνας**	Himonas
In spring	**Την άνοιξη**	Tin aniksi
During the summer	**Κατά τη διάρκεια του καλοκαιριού**	Kata ti dhiarkia tou kalokeriou

YEAR

This year	**Φέτος**	Fetos
Last year	**Πέρσυ**	Persi
Next year	**Του χρόνου**	Tou hronou

PUBLIC HOLIDAYS

1 January: New Year's Day	**1 Ιανουαρίου – Πρωτοχρονιά**	Proti ianouariou – protohronia
25 March: Independence Day	**25 Μαρτίου**	Ikosti pempti martiou
Easter	**Το Άγιον Πάσχα**	To aghion pasha
15 August: The Annunciation	**15 Αυγούστου – Της Παναγίας**	Dekati pempti avghoustou – tis panaghias
28 October: The *Ochi* day (Greece's refusal to surrender to Italy in 1940)	**28 Οκτωβρίου**	Ikosti oghdhoi oktovriou
25 December: Christmas	**25 Δεκεμβρίου – Χριστούγεννα**	Ikosti pempti dhekemvriou – hristoughena
31 December: New Year's Eve	**31 Δεκεμβρίου – Παραμονή Πρωτοχρονιάς**	Triakosti proti dhekemvriou – paramoni protohronias

NUMBERS

CARDINAL

0	**Μηδέν**	Midhen
1	**Ένα**	Ena
2	**Δύο**	Dhio
3	**Τρία**	Tria
4	**Τέσσερα**	Tessera
5	**Πέντε**	Pente
6	**Έξη**	Eksi
7	**Επτά**	Epta
8	**Οκτώ**	Okto
9	**Εννέα**	Enea
10	**Δέκα**	Dheka
11	**Ένδεκα**	Endheka

12	Δώδεκα	Dhodheka
13	Δεκατρία	Dhekatria
14	Δεκατέσσερα	Dhekatessera
15	Δεκαπέντε	Dhekapente
16	Δεκαέξη	Dhekaeksi
17	Δεκαεπτά	Dhekaepta
18	Δεκαοκτώ	Dhekaokto
19	Δεκαεννέα	Dhekaenea
20	Είχοσι	Ikossi
21	Εικοσιένα	Ikossiena
22	Εικοσιδύο	Ikossidhio
30	Τριάντα	Trianda
31	Τριανταένα	Triandaena
40	Σαράντα	Saranda
50	Πενήντα	Peninda
60	Εξήντα	Eksinda
70	Εβδομήντα	Evdhominda
80	Ογδόντα	Oghdhonda
90	Ενενήντα	Eneninda
100	Εκατό	Ekato
101	Εκατονένα	Ekatonena
200	Διακόσια	Dhiakossia
1,000	Χίλια	Hilia
2,000	Δύο χιλιάδες	Dhio hiliadhes
1,000,000	Ένα εκατομμύριο	Ena ekatomirio

ORDINAL

1st	Πρώτος	Protos
2nd	Δεύτερος	Dhefteros
3rd	Τρίτος	Tritos
4th	Τέταρτος	Tetartos
5th	Πέμπτος	Pemptos
6th	Έκτος	Ektos
7th	Έβδομος	Evdhomos
8th	Όγδοος	Oghdhoos
9th	Ένατος	Enatos
10th	Δέκατος	Dhekatos
11th	Ενδέκατος	Endhekatos
12th	Δωδέκατος	Dhodhekatos
13th	Δέκατος τρίτος	Dhekatos tritos
14th	Δέκατος τέταρτος	Dhekatos tetartos
15th	Δέκατος πέμπτος	Dhekatos pemptos
16th	Δέκατος έκτος	Dhekatos ektos
17th	Δέκατος έβδομος	Dhekatos evdhomos
18th	Δέκατος όγδοος	Dhekatos oghdhoos
19th	Δέκατος ένατος	Dhekatos enatos
20th	Είκοστός	Ikostos
21st	Είκοστός πρώτος	Ikostos protos
30th	Τριακοστός	Triakostos
40th	Τεσσαρακοστός	Tessarakostos
50th	Πεντηκοστός	Pentikostos

60th	**Εξηκοστός**	Eksikostos
70th	**Εβδομηκοστός**	Evdhomikostos
80th	**Ογδοηκοστός**	Oghdhoikostos
90th	**Ενενηκοστός**	Enenikostos
100th	**Εκατοστός**	Ekatostos
Half	**Μισός**	Missos
Quarter	**Εν τέταρτον**	En tetarton
Three quarters	**Τρία τέταρτα**	Tria tetarta
A third	**Εν τρίτον**	En triton
Two thirds	**Δύο τρίτα**	Dhio trita

WEIGHTS & MEASURES

DISTANCE

kilometres – miles

km	miles or km	miles	km	miles or km	miles
1·6	1	0·6	14·5	9	5·6
3·2	2	1·2	16·1	10	6·2
4·8	3	1·9	32·2	20	12·4
6·4	4	2·5	40·2	25	15·5
8	5	3·1	80·5	50	31·1
9·7	6	3·7	160·9	100	62·1
11·3	7	4·3	804·7	500	310·7
12·9	8	5·0			

A rough way to convert from miles to km: divide by 5 and multiply by 8; from km to miles, divide by 8 and multiply by 5.

LENGTH AND HEIGHT

centimetres – inches

cm	ins or cm	ins	cm	ins or cm	ins
2·5	1	0·4	17·8	7	2·8
5·1	2	0·8	20·3	8	3·1
7·6	3	1·2	22·9	9	3·5
10·2	4	1·6	25·4	10	3·9
12·7	5	2·0	50·8	20	7·9
15·2	6	2·4	127·0	50	19·7

A rough way to convert from inches to cm: divide by 2 and multiply by 5; from cm to inches: divide by 5 and multiply by 2.

metres – feet

m	ft or m	ft	m	ft or m	ft
0·3	1	3·3	2·4	8	26·2
0·6	2	6·6	2·7	9	29·5
0·9	3	9·8	3	10	32·8
1·2	4	13·1	6·1	20	65·6
1·5	5	16·4	15·2	50	164·0
1·8	6	19·7	30·5	100	328·1
2·1	7	23·0			

A rough way to convert from ft to m: divide by 10 and multiply by 3; from m to ft: divide by 3 and multiply by 10.

metres – yards

m	yds or m	yds	m	yds or m	yds
0·9	1	1·1	7·3	8	8·7
1·8	2	2·2	8·2	9	9·8
2·7	3	3·3	9·1	10	10·9
3·7	4	4·4	18·3	20	21·9
4·6	5	5·5	45·7	50	54·7
5·5	6	6·6	91·4	100	109·4
6·4	7	7·7	457·2	500	456·8

A rough way to convert from yds to m: subtract 10 per cent from the number of yds; from m to yds: add 10 per cent to the number of metres.

LIQUID MEASURES

litres – gallons

litres	galls or litres	galls	litres	galls or litres	galls
4·6	1	0·2	36·4	8	1·8
9·1	2	0·4	40·9	9	2·0
13·6	3	0·7	45·5	10	2·2
18·2	4	0·9	90·9	20	4·4
22·7	5	1·1	136·4	30	6·6
27·3	6	1·3	181·8	40	8·8
31·8	7	1·5	227·3	50	11·0

1 pint = 0·6 litre   1 litre = 1·8 pints

A rough way to convert from galls to litres: divide by 2 and multiply by 9; from litres to galls: divide by 9 and multiply by 2.

WEIGHT 5

kilogrammes – pounds

kg	lb or kg	lb	kg	lb or kg	lb
0·5	1	2·2	3·2	7	15·4
0·9	2	4·4	3·6	8	17·6
1·4	3	6·6	4·1	9	19·8
1·8	4	8·8	4·5	10	22·0
2·3	5	11·0	9·1	20	44·1
2·7	6	13·2	22·7	50	110·2

A rough way to convert from lb to kg: divide by 11 and multiply by 5; from kg to lb: divide by 5 and multiply by 11.

grammes – ounces

grammes	oz	oz	grammes
100	3·5	2	56·7
250	8·8	4	113·4
500	17·6	8	226·8
1,000 (1 kg)	35·2	16 (1 lb)	453·6

TEMPERATURE

centrigrade (°C) – fahrenheit (°F)

°C	°F	°C	°F
−10	14	30	86·0
− 5	23	35	95·0
0	32	37	98·6
5	41	38	100·4
10	50	39	102·2
15	59	40	104·0
20	68	100	212·0
25	77		

To convert °F to °C: deduct 32, divide by 9, multiply by 5; to convert °C to °F: divide by 5, multiply by 9, and add 32.

BASIC GRAMMAR

NOUNS AND ARTICLES

All Greek nouns are divided into three genders: masculine, feminine and neuter.

All nouns of all genders have cases according to their function in a sentence. In addition to the nominative there are also the genitive and the accusative. The genitive expresses possession; the accusative is used after prepositions and as the object of verbs. Articles take the same case as the noun to which they belong.

SINGULAR

Masculine nouns are preceded by the definite article ο (o). Their indefinite article is ένας (enas). They are divided into three groups according to their endings, which are -ος, -ας, -ης; e.g. ο θεός (o theos – the god), ο αέρας (o aeras – the wind), ο εργάτης (o erghatis – the worker).

			-ος		**-ας**		**-ης**	
nom.	**ο**	o	θεός	theos	αέρας	aeras	εργάτης	erghatis
gen.	**του**	tou	θεού	theou	αέρα	aera	εργάτη	erghati
acc.	**τον**	ton	θεό	theo	αέρα	aera	εργάτη	erghati

Feminine nouns are preceded by the definite article η (i). Their indefinite article is μία (mia). They are divided into two groups according to their endings, which are -η and -α; e.g. η ψυχή (i psihi – the soul), η θάλασσα, (i thalassa – the sea).

			-η		**-α**	
nom.	**η**	i	ψυχή	psihi	θάλασσα	thalassa
gen.	**της**	tis	ψυχής	psihis	θάλασσας	thalassas
acc.	**την**	tin	ψυχή	psihi	θάλασσα	thalassa

Neuter nouns are preceded by the definite article το (to), and their indefinite article is ένα (ena). They end mostly in -ο, -α, and -ι; e.g. το πλοίο (to plio – the boat), το δίπλωμα (to dhiploma – the diploma), το τραγούδι (to traghoudhi – the song).

		-ο	**-α**	**-ι**
nom.	**το**	πλοίο	δίπλωμα	τραγούδι
	to	plio	dhiploma	traghoudhi
gen.	**του**	πλοίου	διπλώματος	τραγουδιού
	tou	pliou	dhiplomatos	traghoudhiou
acc.	**το**	πλοίο	δίπλωμα	τραγούδι
	to	plio	dhiploma	traghoudhi

Proper nouns also take an article and have cases, whether they are masculine, feminine or neuter (some names of places only).

PLURAL

Masculine The article ο changes to οί. Masculine nouns ending in -ος change to -οι; those ending in -ας and -ης to -ες.

	-οι			**-ες**	**-ες**		
nom.	**οι**	i	**θεοί**	thei	αέρες	aeres	εργάτες	erghates
gen.	**των**	ton	**θεών**	theon	αέρων	aeron	εργατών	erghaton
acc.	**τούς**	tous	**θεούς**	theous	αέρες	aeres	εργάτες	erghates

Feminine The article η changes to οι. The ending -η or -α changes to -ες. Some feminine nouns change the ending -η to -εις; e.g. η πόλη (i poli – the town) becomes οι πόλεις (i polis – the towns); η λέξη (i leksi – the word), οι λέξεις (i leksis – the words).

			-ες		**-εις**	
nom.	**οι**	i	**ψυχές**	psihes	πόλεις	polis
gen.	**των**	ton	**ψυχών**	psihon	πόλεων	poleon
acc.	**τίς**	tis	**ψυχές**	psihes	πόλεις	polis

Neuter The article το changes to τα. The ending -ο changes to -α, the ending -α to -ατα, the ending -ι to -ια.

			-α	**-ατα**	**-ια**
nom.	**τα**	πλοία	διπλώματα	τραυούδια
	ta	plia	dhiplomata	traghoudhia
gen.	**των**	πλοίων	διπλωμάτων	τραγουδιών
	ton	plion	dhiplomaton	traghoudhion
acc.	**τα**	πλοία	διπλώματα	τραγούδια
	ta	plia	dhiplomata	traghoudhia

ADJECTIVES

The endings of adjectives correspond to the three genders of the nouns they qualify. Masculine adjectives end in -ος (plural -οι); e.g. ο καλός – good. Feminine adjectives end in -η and some in -α (plural -ες); e.g. η καλή – good. Neuter adjectives end in -ο (plural -α); e.g. το καλό – good. Masculine, feminine and neuter adjectives have the same three cases (nominative, genitive and accusative) as the nouns they qualify.

For example:

	Masculine	**Feminine**	**Neuter**
nom.	ο καλός	η καλή	το καλό
	o kalos	i kali	to kalo
gen.	του καλού	της καλής	του καλού
	tou kalou	tis kalis	tou kalou
acc.	τον καλό	την καλή	το καλό
	ton kalo	tin kali	to kalo

Adjectives usually precede the nouns they qualify.

Possessive adjectives follow the nouns with which they are associated and they change for person and number. They are not stressed.

Singular		**Plural**	
μου	mou (*my*)	μας	mas (*our*)
σου	sou (*your*)	σας	sas (*your*)
του	tou (*his*)	τους	tous (*their*)
της	tis (*hers*)		
του	tou (*its*)		
ο άντρας μου	(*my husband*)	οι άντρες μας	(*our husbands*)
o **andras** mou		i **andres** mas	
η γυναίκα σου	(*your wife*)	οι γυναίκες σας	(*your wives*)
i **ghineka** sou		i **ghinekes** sas	
το παιδί του/της	his/her child	τα παιδιά τους	(*their children*)
to **pedhi** tou/tis		ta **pedhia** tous	

PRONOUNS

Possessive pronouns have the same gender and number as the nouns they replace.

MASCULINE

Singular		**Plural**	
δικός μου	*mine*	δικός μας	*ours*
	(*i.e. this ... is mine*)		(*i.e. this ... is ours*)
δικός σου	*yours*	δικός σας	*yours*
δικός του	*his*	δικός τους	*theirs*
δικός της	*hers*		
δικός του	*its*		

FEMININE

NEUTER

Singular	**Plural**	**Singular**	**Plural**
δική μου, etc.	δικές μου	δικό μου, etc.	δικά μας
(*i.e. this ... is mine*)		(*i.e. this ... is mine*)	

In the case of plural possession (i.e. the possession of more than one object) the masculine δικός changes to δικοί, the feminine δική to δικές and the neuter δικό to δικά, just as with nouns.

δικοί μας   (*i.e. these ... are ours*)
δικές μου   (*i.e. these ... are mine*)
δικά του   (*i.e. these ... are his*)

PERSONAL PRONOUNS:

εγώ	egho	*I*	εμείς	emis	*we*
εσύ	essi	*you*	εσείς	essis	*you*
αυτός	aftos	*he*	αυτοί	afti	*they*
αυτή	afti	*she*			
αυτό	afto	*it*			

As the endings of verbs denote person, it is not necessary to use the personal pronouns except for emphasis.

The object (accusative) pronouns:

αυτόν	afton	*him*	αυτούς	aftous	*them (m)*
αυτήν	aftin	*her*	αυτές	aftes	*them (f)*
αυτό	afto	*it*	αυτά	afta	*them (n)*

Nouns which are used as objects of verbs can be replaced by the above pronouns.

VERBS

To Be

Present		Past and Imperfect		Future	
είμαι	*I am*	ήμουν	*I was, etc.*	θά ειμαι	*I shall be*
είσαι	*you are*	ήσουν	*you were*	θά εισαι	*you will be*
είναι	*he/she/ it is*	ήταν	*he/she/ it was*	θά είναι	*he/she/ it will be*
είμαστε	*we are*	ήμασταν	*we were*	θά είμαστε	*we shall be*
είσαστε	*you are*	ήσασταν	*you were*	θά είστε	*you will be*
είναι	*they are*	ήταν	*they were*	θά είναι	*they will be*

To have

Present		Past and Imperfect		Future	
έχω	*I have*	είχα	*I had*	θά έχω	*I shall have*
έχεις	*you have*	είχες	*you had*	θά έχεις	*you will have*
έχει	*he/she/ it has*	είχε	*he/she/. it had*	θά έχει	*he/she/ it will have*
έχουμε	*we have*	είχαμε	*we had*	θά έχουμε	*we shall have*
έχετε	*you have*	είχατε	*you had*	θά έχετε	*you will have*
έχουν	*they have*	είχαν	*they had*	θά έχουν	*they will have*

REGULAR VERBS

Greek regular verbs may be *active*, ending in -ω in the first person singular of the present tense and denoting an action performed by the subject, or *passive*, ending in -μαι in the first person singular of the present tense and denoting an action received by the subject. This division, however, is only a general one and it does not necessarily apply in all cases. Most verbs have both active and passive forms.

The **present tense** corresponds to the English simple present and the present continuous (I do, I am doing).

Active		*Passive*	
πλένω	*I wash, etc.*	πλένομαι	*I wash myself, etc.*
πλένεις		πλένεσαι	
πλένει		πλένεται	
πλένουμε		πλενόμαστε	
πλένετε		πλενόσαστε	
πλένουν		πλένονται	

The **future tense** is formed by placing the particle θά in front of the indefinite, which is otherwise never used by itself. By placing the particle θά in front of the present tense, one expresses the future continuous (I shall be doing). The indefinite is more or less the same as the English infinitive, but it is conjugated. As there are nine sub-classes of active verbs, depending on the way the indefinite is formed, and as it will be practically impossible for users of this book to familiarize themselves sufficiently with all the verbs that fall under these classes, it will be enough here to give only a few examples.

θά αρχίσω	*I shall begin, etc.*	θά δουλέψω	*I shall work, etc.*	θά κάνω	*I shall make, etc.*
θά αρχίσης		θά δουλέψης		θά κάνης	
θά αρχίση		θά δουλέψη		θά κάνη	
θά αρχίσωμε		θά δουλέψωμε		θά κάνωμε	
θά αρχίσετε		θά δουλέψετε		θά κάνετε	
θά αρχίσουν		θά δουλέψουν		θά κάνουν	

The *past tense* is formed by changing the final -ω of the indefinite to -α. As in the case of the future tense, unless one is familiar with the indefinite forms, it is impossible to give a simple rule in forming the simple past.

The *imperfect tense* is formed by using the present, instead of the indefinite, but otherwise changing the ending as in the past tense.

Past		Imperfect	
άρχισα	I began, etc.	άρχιζα	I was beginning, etc.
άρχισες		άρχιζες	
άρχισε		άρχιζε	
αρχίσαμε		αρχίζαμε	
αρχίσατε		αρχίζατε	
αρχισαν		αρχιζαν	

The *perfect tenses* are formed by the auxiliary verb έχω (I have) in the present and είχα (I had) in the past with the third person singular of the indefinite.

Present perfect		Past perfect	
έχω άρχίσει	I have begun, etc.	είχα αρχίσει	I had begun, etc.
έχεις άρχίσει		είχες αρχίσει	
έχει αρχίσει		είχε αρχίσει	
έχουμε άρχίσει		είχαμε αρχίσει	
έχετε άρχίσει		είχατε αρχίσει	
έχουν άρχίσει		είχαν αρχίσει	

The *imperative form*, which expresses command or request in the second person, is formed by changing the -ω of the indefinite into -ε.

indefinite	imperative
αρχίσω	αρχισε
παίξω	παίξε
γράψω	γράψε

PREPOSITIONS

σ' (σε)	se	*to (person or object)*
στόν **masc.**	ston	*to (direction), at*
στή(ν) **fem.**	sti(n)	
στό **neut.**	sto	
χωρίς	horis	*without*
γιά	ghia	*for*
προς	pros	*towards*
πρίν	prin	*before*
με	me	*with*
από	apo	*from*
ως	os	*until*
μέχρι	mehri	*until*
μετά	meta	*after*
σάν	san	*like*
παρά	para	*in spite of*
πάνω στό	pano sto	*on*
κοντά στό	konda sto	*near*
μέσα στό	messa sto	*in*
γύρω στό	ghiro sto	*around*
μαζί μέ	mazi me	*with*
πάνω από	pano apo	*over*
κάτω από	kato apo	*under*
πίσω από	pisso apo	*behind*
γύρω σέ	ghiro se	*around (time)*
γύρω από	ghiro apo	*round*
έξω από	ekso apo	*outside of*
πρίν από	prin apo	*before*
ίστερα από	istera apo	*after*

VOCABULARY

Various groups of specialized words are given elsewhere in this book and these words are not usually repeated in the Vocabulary:

Adjectives are given here in their masculine form. Verbs are given in the first person singular of the present tense.

A

a, an *masc., fem., neut.*	ένας, μία, ένα	enas, mia, ena
abbey	μονή	moni
able (to be)	μπορώ	boro
about	περίπου	peripou
above	από πάνω	apo pano
abroad	εξωτερικό	eksoteriko
accept (to)	δέχομαι	dhehome
accident	ατύχημα	atihima
accommodation	στέγαση	steghassi
account	λογαριασμός	loghariasmos
ache (to)	πονώ	pono
acquaintance	γνωριμία	ghnorimia
across	απέναντι	apenandi
act (to)	ενεργώ	energho
add (to)	προσθέτω	prostheto
address	διεύθυνση	dhiefthinssi
admire (to)	θαυμάζω	thavmazo
adventure	περιπέτεια	peripetia
advertisement	διαφήμιση	dhiafimissi
advice	συμβουλή	simvouli
aeroplane	αεροπλάνο	aeroplano
afford (to)	διαθέτω	dhiatheto
afraid (to be)	φοβάμαι	fovame

after	μετά	meta
afternoon	απόγευμα	apoghevma
again	ξανά	ksana
against	εναντίον	enantion
age	ηλικία	ilikia
ago	προ, πριν	pro, prin
agree (to)	συμφωνώ	simfono
ahead	εμπρός	embros
air	αέρας	aeras
air-conditioning	κλιματισμός	klimatismos
alarm clock	ξυπνητήρι	ksipnitiri
alcoholic (drink)	αλκοολικό (ποτό)	alkoöliko (poto)
alike	όμοιος	omios
alive	ζωντανός	zontanos
all	όλοι	oli
all right	εντάξει	endaksi
allow (to)	επιτρέπω	epitrepo
almost	σχεδόν	skhedhon
alone	μόνος	monos
along	κατά μήκος	kata mikos
already	ήδη	idhi
also	επίσης	epissis
alter (to)	αλλάζω	alazo
alternative	άλλος	allos
although	αν και	an ke
always	πάντα	panda

ambulance	**νοσοκομειακό αυτοκίνητο**	nossokomiako aftokinito
American *adj.*	**Αμερικανικός**	amerikanikos
American *noun*	**Αμερικάνος**	amerikanos
among	**μεταξύ**	metaksi
amuse (to)	**διασκεδάζω**	dhiaskedhazo
amusement park	**λουναπάρκ**	lounapark
amusing	**διασκεδαστικό**	dhiaskedhastiko
ancient	**αρχαίος**	arheos
and	**και**	ke
angry	**θυμωμένος**	thimomenos
animal	**ζώον**	zoön
anniversary	**επέτειος**	epetios
annoy (to)	**ενοχλώ**	enohlo
annoyed	**ενοχλημένος**	enohlimenos
another *masc., fem., neut.*	**ένας άλλος, άλλη, άλλο**	efas alos, ali, alo
answer	**απάντηση**	apantissi
answer (to)	**απαντώ**	apando
antique	**αντίκες**	antikes
any	**κάθε**	kathe
anyone *masc., fem., neut.*	**οποιοσδήποτε, οποιαδήποτε, οποιοδήποτε**	opiosdhipote, opiadhipote, opiodhipote
anything	**οτιδήποτε**	otidhipote
anyway	**έτσι κι αλλιώς**	etsi ki alios
anywhere	**οπουδήποτε**	opoudhipote

apartment	**διαμέρισμα**	dhiamerisma
apologize (to)	**ζητώ συγγνώμη**	zito sighnomi
appetite	**όρεξη**	oreksi
architect	**αρχιτέκτονας**	arhitektonas
architecture	**αρχιτεκτονική**	arhitektoniki
area	**περιοχή**	periohi
area code	**κωδικός**	kodhikos
argument *quarrel*	**καβγάς**	kavghas
argument *reason*	**επιχείρημα**	epihirima
arm	**μπράτσο**	bratso
armchair	**πολυθρόνα**	polithrona
army	**στρατός**	stratos
around	**τριγύρω**	trighiro
arrange (to)	**τακτοποιώ**	taktopio
arrival	**άφιξη**	afiksi
arrive (to)	**φθάνω**	fthano
art	**τέχνη**	tehni
art gallery	**πινακοθήκη**	pinakothiki
artificial	**τεχνητός**	tehnitos
artist	**καλλιτέχνης**	kalitehnis
as	**σαν**	san
as much as	**τόσο όσο**	tosso osso
as soon as	**μόλις**	molis
as well/also	**επίσης**	epissis
ashtray	**τασάκι**	tasaki
ask (to)	**ρωτώ**	roto

asleep	**κοιμισμένος**	kimismenos
at	**στο**	sto
at last	**επιτέλους**	epitelous
at once	**αμέσως**	amessos
atmosphere	**ατμόσφαιρα**	atmosfera
attention	**προσοχή**	prossohi
attractive	**ελκυστικός**	elkistikos
auction	**πλειστηριασμός**	plistiriazmos
audience	**ακροατήριο**	akroatirio
aunt	**θεία**	thia
Australia	**Αυστραλία**	afstralia
Australian	**Αυστραλός**	afstralos
author	**συγγραφέας**	singhrafeas
autumn	**φθινόπωρο**	fthinoporo
available	**διαθέσιμος**	dhiathessimos
avenue	**λεωφόρος**	leoforos
average	**μέσος**	messos
avoid (to)	**αποφεύγω**	apofevgho
awake (to)	**ξυπνώ**	ksipno
away *far*	**μακρυά**	makria
awful	**φοβερός**	foveros

B

baby	**μωρό**	moro
baby food	**παιδικές τροφές**	pedhikes trofes
baby-sitter	**μπέϊμπισιτερ**	baby-sitter

bachelor	εργένης	erghenis
back *adv.*	πίσω	pisso
bad	κακός	kakos
bad (food)	χαλασμένο (φαγητό)	halasmeno (faghito)
bag	τσάντα	tsanta
baggage	αποσκευή	aposkevi
baggage cart	τρόλλευ καρότσι αποσκευών	trolli karotsi aposkevon
baggage check	έλεγχος αποσκευών	elenhos aposkevon
bait	δόλωμα	dholoma
balcony	μπαλκόνι	balkoni
ball *sport*	μπάλα	bala
ballet	μπαλλέτο	baleto
balloon	μπαλόνι	baloni
band *music*	μπάντα	banda
bank account	λογαριασμός τράπεζας	loghariasmos trapezas
barbecue	ψησταριά	psistaria
barber	κουρέας	koureas
bare	γυμνός	ghimnos
barn	αχυρώνας	ahironas
basket	καλάθι	kalathi
bath	μπάνιο	banio
bath essence	άρωμα μπάνιου	aroma baniou
bathe (to)	πλένομαι	plenome
bathing cap	σκούφια κολυμπήματος	skoufia kolimbimatos

bathing costume/ trunks	μαγιώ	maghio
bathroom	μπάνιο	banio
battery	μπαταρία	bataria
bay	κόλπος	kolpos
be (to)	είμαι	ime
beach	αμμουδιά, παραλία	amoudhia, paralia
beard	γενειάδα	gheniadha
beautiful	ωραίος	oreos
because	γιατί	ghiati
become (to)	γίνομαι	ghinome
bed	κρεββάτι	krevati
bed and breakfast	δωμάτιο με πρωινό	dhomatio me proino
bedroom	κρεββατοκάμαρα	krevatokamara
before	πριν	prin
begin (to)	αρχίζω	arhizo
beginning	αρχή	arhi
behind	από πίσω	apo pisso
believe (to)	πιστεύω	pistevo
bell	κουδούνι	koudhouni
belong (to)	ανήκω	aniko
below	από κάτω	apo kato
belt	ζώνη	zoni
bench	πάγκος	pangos
bend (to)	σκύβω	skivo
beneath	από κάτω	apo kato

berth	κουκέτα	kouketa
beside	πλάι	plai
best	ο καλύτερος	o kaliteros
bet	στοίχημα	stihima
better	καλύτερος	kaliteros
between	ανάμεσα/μεταξύ	anamessa/metaksi
beyond	πέραν	peran
bicycle	ποδήλατο	podhilato
big	μεγάλος	meghalos
bill	λογαριασμός	loghariasmos
binoculars	κιάλια	kialia
bird	πουλί	pouli
birthday	γενέθλια	ghenethlia
bite (to)	δαγκώνω	dhangono
bitter	πικρός	pikros
blanket	κουβέρτα	kouverta
bleed (to)	ματώνω	matono
blind	τυφλός	tiflos
blister	φουσκάλα	fouskala
blond	ξανθός	ksanthos
blood	αίμα	ema
blouse	μπλούζα	blouza
blow	γροθιά	ghrothia
blow (to)	φυσώ	fisso
(on) board	επάνω στο πλοίο	epano sto plio
boarding house	πανσιόν	pansion

boat *rowing boat*	**βάρκα**	varka
boat *steamer*	**πλοίο**	plio
body	**σώμα**	soma
bone	**κόκκαλο**	kokalo
bonfire	**φωτιά**	fotia
book	**βιβλίο**	vivlio
book (to)	**κλείνω**	klino
boot	**μπότα**	bota
border	**σύνορο**	sinoro
bored	**βαρεμένος**	varemenos
boring	**βαρετός**	varetos
borrow (to)	**δανείζομαι**	dhanizome
both	**και οι δύο**	ke i dhio
bother (to) *annoy*	**ενοχλώ**	enohlo
bottle	**μπουκάλι**	boukali
bottle opener	**τιρμπουσόν**	tirbousson
bottom	**πάτος**	patos
bow tie	**παπιγιόν**	papighion
bowl	**γαβάδα**	ghavatha
box *container*	**κουτί**	kouti
box *theatre*	**θεωρείο**	theorio
box office	**ταμείο**	tamio
boy	**αγόρι**	aghori
bracelet	**βραχιόλι**	vrahioli
braces	**τιράντες**	tirantes
brain	**μυαλό**	mialo

branch *section of*	**τμήμα**	tmima
branch *of a tree*	**κλαδί**	kladhi
brand	**μάρκα**	marka
brassière	**σουτιέν**	soutien
break (to)	**σπάζω**	spazo
breakfast	**πρόγευμα**	proghevma
breathe (to)	**αναπνέω**	anapneo
brick	**τούβλο**	touvlo
bridge	**γέφυρα**	ghefira
bridge *game*	**μπρίτξ**	bridge
briefs	**σώβρακα**	sovraka
bright	**λαμπερός**	lamberos
bring (to)	**φέρνω**	ferno
British	**Βρεταννικός**	vretanikos
broken	**σπασμένος**	spasmenos
brooch/buckle	**αγκράφα**	agrafa
broom	**σκούπα**	skoupa
brother	**αδελφός**	adhelfos
bruise (to)	**μελανιάζω**	melaniazo
brush	**βούρτσα**	vourtsa
brush (to)	**βουρτσίζω**	vourtsizo
bucket	**κουβάς**	kouvas
build (to)	**κτίζω**	ktizo
building	**κτίριο**	ktirio
bunch *flowers*	**μάτσο**	matso
buoy	**σημαδούρα**	simadhoura

burn (to)	καίω	keo
burst (to) *storm*	ξεσπάω	ksespao
bus	λεωφορείο	leoforio
bus stop	στάσις λεωφορείου	stassis leoforiou
business	επιχείρησις	epihirissis
busy	απασχολημένος	apaskholimenos
but	αλλά	ala
butterfly	πεταλούδα	petaloudha
button	κουμπί	koumbi
buy (to)	αγοράζω	aghorazo
by	από	apo

C

cabin	καμπίνα	kabina
calculator	υπολογιστική μηχανή	ipologhistiki mihani
calendar	ημερολόγιο	imerologhio
call (to) *name*	ονομάζω	onomazo
call (to) *shout, cry*	φωνάζω	fonazo
call (to) *summon*	καλώ	kalo
call *telephone*	τηλεφώνημα	tilefonima
call (to) *telephone*	τηλεφωνώ	tilefono
call *visit*	επίσκεψη	episkepsi
call (to) *visit*	επισκέπτομαι	episkeptome
calm	ήρεμος	iremos

camera	**φωτογραφική μηχανή**	fotoghrafiki mihani
camp (to)	**κατασκηνώνω**	kataskinono
camp site	**χώρος κατασκηνώσεως**	horos kataskinoseos
can (to be able)	**μπορώ**	boro
can (tin)	**κονσέρβα**	konserva
can opener	**ανοικτήρι γιά κονσέρβες**	aniktiri ghia konserves
Canada	**Καναδάς**	kanadhas
Canadian	**Καναδός**	kanadhos
cancel (to)	**ακυρώνω**	akirono
candle	**κερί**	keri
canoe	**κανό**	kano
cap	**σκούφια**	skoufia
capable	**ικανός**	ikanos
capital *city*	**πρωτεύουσα**	protevoussa
car	**αυτοκίνητο**	aftokinito
car park	**χώρος σταθμεύσεως αυτοκινήτων**	horos stathmefseos aftokiniton
carafe	**καράφα**	karafa
care	**φροντίδα**	frontidha
careful	**προσεκτικός**	prosektikos
careless	**απρόσεκτος**	aprosektos
caretaker	**θυρωρός**	thiroros
carpet	**χαλί**	hali
carry (to)	**κουβαλώ**	kouvalo

cash	μετρητά	metrita
cash (to)	εξαργυρώνω	exarghirono
cashier	ταμίας	tamias
casino	kazíno	kazino
cassette	κασσέττα	kasseta
cassette recorder	κασσεττόφωνο	kassetofono
castle	κάστρο	kastro
cat	γάτα	ghata
catalogue	κατάλογος	kataloghos
catch (to)	πιάνω	piano
cathedral	μητρόπολις	mitropolis
catholic	καθολικός	katholikos
cause	αιτία	etia
cave	σπηλιά	spilia
cement	τσιμέντο	tsimendo
central	κεντρικός	kentrikos
centre	κέντρο	kentro
century	αιώνας	eonas
ceremony	τελετή	teleti
certain	βέβαιος	veveos
certainly	βεβαίως	veveos
chain *jewellery*	αλυσίδα	alissidha
chair	καρέκλα	karekla
chambermaid	καμαριέρα	kamariera
chance *luck*	τύχη	tihi
(small) change	ψιλά	psila

change (to)	αλλάζω	alazo
chapel	παρεκκλήσι	pareklissi
charge	τιμή	timi
charge (to)	χρεώνω	hreono
cheap	φτηνό	ftino
check (to)	ελέγχω	elenho
cheque	επιταγή	epitaghi
chess/chess set	σκάκι	skaki
child	παιδί	pedhi
chill (to)	ψυχραίνω	psihreno
china	πιατικά	piatika
choice	εκλογή	ekloghi
choose (to)	διαλέγω	dhialegho
church	εκκλησία	eklissia
cigarette case	τσιγαροθήκη	tsigharothiki
cine camera	κινηματογραφική μηχανή	kinimatoghrafiki mihani
cinema	κινηματόγραφος	kinimatoghrafos
circle *theatre*	εξώστης	eksostis
circus	τσίρκο	tsirko
city	πόλη	poli
class	τάξη	taksi
clean	καθαρός	katharos
clean (to)	καθαρίζω	katharizo
cleansing cream	κρέμα καθαρίσμού προσώπου	krema katharismou prossopou
clear	καθαρός	katharos

clerk	υπάλληλος	ipalilos
cliff	γκρεμνός	gremnos
climb (to)	σκαρφαλώνω	skarfalono
cloakroom	γκαρνταρόμπα	gardaroba
clock	ρολόϊ	roloi
close (to)	κλείνω	klino
closed	κλειστό	klisto
cloth/fabric	ύφασμα	ifasma
clothes	ρούχα	rouha
cloud	σύννεφο	sinefo
coach	λεωφορείο	leoforio
coast	ακτή	akti
coat	παλτό	palto
coat hanger	κρεμάστρα	kremastra
coin	νόμισμα	nomisma
cold *adj.*	κρύο	krio
collar	κολλάρο	kolaro
collar stud	κουμπί κολλάρου	koumbi kolarou
collect (to)	μαζεύω	mazevo
colour	χρώμα	hroma
comb	κτένι	kteni
come (to)	έρχομαι	erhome
come in (to)	μπαίνω	beno
comfortable	αναπαυτικός	anapaftikos
common	κοινός	kinos
company *business*	εταιρεία	eteria

compartment *train*	**διαμέρισμα τραίνου**	dhiamerisma trenou
compass	**πυξίδα**	piksidha
compensation	**αποζημίωση**	apozimiossi
complain (to)	**διαμαρτύρομαι**	dhiamartirome
complaint	**παράπονο**	parapono
complete	**πλήρες**	plires
completely	**τελείως**	telios
computer	**υπολογιστής**	ipologhistis
concert	**συναυλία**	sinavlia
concert hall	**αίθουσα συναυλιών**	ethoussa sinavlion
concrete *cement*	**τσιμέντο**	tsimendo
concrete *specific*	**συγκεκριμένος**	singekrimenos
conductor *bus*	**εισπράκτωρ**	ispraktor
conductor *orchestra*	**μαέστρος**	maestros
congratulations	**συγχαρητήρια**	sinharitiria
connect (to)	**συνδέω**	sindheo
connection *train, etc.*	**ανταπόκριση**	antapokrissi
consul	**πρόξενος**	proksenos
consulate	**προξενείο**	proksenio
contact lens	**φακοί επαφής**	faki epafis
contain (to)	**περιέχω**	perieho
contraceptive	**προφυλακτικό**	profilaktiko
convenient	**βολικός**	volikos
convent	**μοναστήρι**	monastiri
conversation	**συζήτηση**	sizitissi
cook	**μάγειρας**	maghiras

cook (to)	μαγειρεύω	maghirevo
cool	δροσερός	dhrosseros
copper	χαλκός	halkos
copy	αντίγραφο	antighrafo
copy (to)	αντιγράφω	antighrafo
cork	φελλός	felos
corkscrew	τιρμπουσόν	tirbousson
corner	γωνία	ghonia
correct	σωστός	sostos
corridor	διάδρομος	dhiadhromos
cosmetics	καλλυντικά	kalintika
cost	κόστος, τιμή	kostos, timi
cost (to)	κοστίζω	kostizo
costume jewellery	κοσμήματα	kosmimata
cot	κούνια/κρεββατάκι	kounia/krevataki
cottage	σπιτάκι	spitaki
cotton	βαμβακερό	vamvakero
cotton wool	βαμβάκι	vamvaki
couchette	κουκέττα	kouketa
count (to)	μετρώ	metro
country *nation*	χώρα	hora
country *not town*	εξοχή	eksohi
couple	ζευγάρι	zevghari
course *dish*	πιάτο	piato
courtyard	αυλή	avli
cousin	ξάδελφος	ksadhelfos

cover	**σκέπασμα**	skepasma
cover (to)	**σκεπάζω**	skepazo
cow	**αγελάδα**	agheladha
crash *collision*	**σύγκρουση**	singroussi
crease	**τσαλάκωμα**	tsalakoma
credit	**πίστωση**	pistossi
credit card	**κάρτα πιστώσεως**	karta pistoseos
crew	**πλήρωμα**	pliroma
cross *symbol*	**σταυρός**	stavros
cross (to) *traverse*	**διασχίζω**	dhiashizo
crossroads	**σταυροδρόμι**	stavrodhromi
crossword	**σταυρόλεξο**	stavrolekso
crowd	**πλήθος**	plithos
crowded	**γεμάτος κόσμο**	ghematos kosmo
cry (to) *weep*	**κλαίω**	kleo
crystal	**κρύσταλλο**	kristalo
cufflinks	**μανικέτια**	maniketia
cup	**φλυτζάνι**	flidzani
cupboard	**ντουλάπι**	doulapi
cure (to)	**γιατρεύω**	ghiatrevo
curious	**περίεργος**	perierghos
curl	**μπούκλα**	boukla
current	**ρεύμα**	revma
curtain	**κουρτίνα**	kourtina
curve	**καμπή**	kambi
cushion	**μαξιλάρι**	maksilari

customs	τελωνείο	telonio
customs officer	τελωνειακός υπάλληλος	teloniakos ipalilos
cut	κόψιμο	kopsimo
cut (to)	κόβω	kovo
cycling	ποδηλασία	podhilassia
cyclist	ποδηλατιστής	podhilatistis

D

daily	καθημερινά	kathimerina
damaged	χαλασμένος	halasmenos
damp	υγρός	ighros
dance	χορός	horos
dance (to)	χορεύω	horevo
danger	κίνδυνος	kindhinos
dangerous	επικίνδυνος	epikindhinos
dark	σκοτεινός	skotinos
date *appointment*	ραντεβού	rendezvous
date *calendar*	ημερομηνία	imerominia
daughter	κόρη	kori
dawn	ξημέρωμα	ksimeroma
day	ημέρα	imera
dead	νεκρός	nekros
deaf	κουφός	koufos
dealer	έμπορος	emboros
dear *affection*	αγαπητός	aghapitos

decanter	**καράφα**	karafa
decide (to)	**αποφασίζω**	apofassizo
deck	**κατάστρωμα**	katastroma
deckchair	**σεζλονγκ**	chaiz long
declare (to)	**δηλώνω**	dhilono
deep	**βαθύς**	vathis
delay	**αργοπορία**	arghoporia
deliver (to)	**παραδίδω**	paradhidho
delivery	**διανομή**	dhianomi
dentures	**μασέλες**	masseles
deodorant	**αποσμητικό γιά τον ιδρώτα**	aposmitiko ghia ton idhrota
depart (to)	**αναχωρώ**	anahoro
department	**τμήμα**	tmima
departure	**αναχώρηση**	anahorissi
dessert	**γλυκό**	ghliko
detour	**στροφή προς αποφυγήν εμποδίου**	strofi pros apofighin embodhiou
dial (to)	**παίρνω αριθμό τηλεφώνου**	perno arithmo tilefonou
dialling code	**κωδικός τηλεφώνου**	kodhikos tilephonou
diamond	**διαμάντι**	dhiamandi
dice	**ζάρια**	zaria
dictionary	**λεξικό**	leksiko
diet	**δίαιτα**	dhieta
diet (to)	**κάνω δίαιτα**	kano dhieta

different	διαφορετικός	dhiaforetikos
difficult	δύσκολος	dhiskolos
dine (to)	γευματίζω	ghevmatizo
dining room	τραπεζαρία	trapezaria
dinner	δείπνο	dhipno
dinner jacket	σμόκιν	smoking
direct	απ'ευθείας	apefthias
direction	κατεύθυνση	katefthinsi
dirty	βρώμικος	vromikos
disappointment	απογοήτευση	apoghoitefsi
discotheque	ντισκοτέκ	discotheque
discount	έκπτωση	ekptossi
dish	πιάτο	piato
disinfectant	απολυμαντικό	apolimantiko
distance	απόσταση	apostassi
disturb (to)	ανησυχώ	anissiho
ditch	αυλάκι	avlaki
dive (to)	βουτώ	vouto
diving board	εξέδρα γιά βουτιές	eksedhra ghia vouties
divorced	χωρισμένος	horismenos
do (to)	κάνω	kano
dock (to)	πλευρίζω	plevrizo
doctor	γιατρός	ghiatros
dog	σκύλος	skilos
doll	κούκλα	koukla
door	πόρτα	porta

double	διπλός	dhiplos
double bed	διπλό κρεββάτι	dhiplo krevati
double room	διπλό δωμάτιο	dhiplo dhomatio
down(stairs)	κάτω	kato
dozen	δώδεκα	dhodheka
draughty	έχει ρεύμα	ehi revma
draw (to) *picture*	σχεδιάζω	skhedhiazo
drawer	συρτάρι	sirtari
drawing	σχέδιο	skhedhio
dream	όνειρο	oniro
dress	φόρεμα	forema
dressing gown	ρόμπα	roba
dressmaker	ράφτρα	raftra
drink (to)	πίνω	pino
drinking water	πόσιμο νερό	possimo nero
drive (to)	οδηγώ	odhigho
driver	οδηγός	odhighos
driving licence	άδεια οδηγού	adhia odhighou
drop (to)	ρίχνω	rihno
drunk	μεθυσμένος	methismenos
dry *adj.*	στεγνός	steghnos
during	κατά τη διάρκεια	kata ti dhiarkia
dusk	σούρουπο	souroupo
duvet	πάπλωμα	paploma
dye	βαφή	vafi

E

each	κάθε	kathe
early	νωρίς	noris
earrings	σκουλαρίκια	skoularikia
east	ανατολή	anatoli
Easter	Πάσχα	paskha
easy	εύκολος	efkolos
eat (to)	τρώγω	trogho
edge	άκρη	akri
EEC	ΕΟΚ (Κοινή Αγορά)	kini aghora
elastic	ελαστικός	elastikos
electric light bulb	ηλεκτρική λάμπα	ilektriki lamba
electric point	πρίζα	priza
electricity	ηλεκτρισμός	ilektrismos
elevator	ασανσέρ	assanser
embarrass (to)	φέρνω σε αμηχανία	ferno se amihania
embassy	πρεσβεία	presvia
emergency exit	έξοδος κινδύνου	eksodhos kindhinou
empty	άδειος	adhios
end	τέλος	telos
engaged *people*	αρραβωνιασμένος	aravoniasmenos
engaged *telephone*	πιασμένο	piasmeno
engine	μηχανή	mihani
England	Αγγλία	anglia
English	Άγγλος	anglos
enjoy (to)	χαίρομαι	herome

enough	αρκετά	arketa
enquiries	πληροφορίες	plirofories
enter (to)	μπαίνω	beno
entrance/entrance fee	είσοδος	issodhos
equipment	εφόδιο	efodhio
escalator	κυλιόμενη σκάλα	kiliomeni skala
escape (to)	δραπετεύω	dhrapetevo
estate agent	μεσίτης	messitis
Europe	Ευρώπη	evropi
even *not odd*	ζυγός	zighos
evening	βράδυ	vradhi
event	γεγονός	gheghonos
ever	πάντα	panda
every	κάθε	kathe
everybody	όλοι	oli
everything	όλα	ola
everywhere	παντού	pantou
example	παράδειγμα	paradhighma
excellent	θαυμάσιος	thavmassios
except	εκτός	ektos
excess	υπερβολή	ipervoli
exchange *bureau*	τράπεζα	trapeza
exchange rate	τιμή συναλλάγματος	timi sinalaghmatos
excursion	εκδρομή	ekdhromi
excuse	συγγνώμη	sighnomi
exhausted	κατάκοπος	katakopos

exhibition	έκθεση	ekthessi
exit	έξοδος	eksodhos
expect (to)	περιμένω	perimeno
expensive	ακριβός	akrivos
explain (to)	εξηγώ	eksigho
express *post*	κατεπείγον	katepighon
express train	ταχεία	tahia
extra	έξτρα	ekstra
eye shadow	μακιγιάζ ματιών	makighiaz mation

F

fabric	ύφασμα	ifasma
face	πρόσωπο	prossopo
face cloth	πανί προσώπου	pani prossopou
face cream	κρέμα προσώπου	krema prossopou
face powder	πούδρα	poudhra
fact	γεγονός	gheghonos
factory	εργοστάσιο	erghostassio
fade (to)	ξεθωριάζω	ksethoriazo
faint (to)	λιποθυμώ	lipothimo
fair *colour*	ξανθός	ksanthos
fair *fête*	γιορτή	ghiorti
fall (to)	πέφτω	pefto
family	οικογένεια	ikoghenia
far	μακριά	makria
fare	εισιτήριο	issitirio

farm	**κτήμα**	ktima
farmer	**αγρότης**	aghrotis
farmhouse	**οικία αγροκτήματος**	ikia aghroktimatos
farther	**πιό μακριά**	pio makria
fashion	**μόδα**	modha
fast	**γρήγορα**	ghrighora
fat	**παχύς**	pahis
father	**πατέρας**	pateras
fault	**λάθος**	lathos
fear	**φόβος**	fovos
feed (to)	**τρέφω**	trefo
feeding bottle	**μπιμπερό**	bibero
feel (to) *emotion*	**αισθάνομαι**	esthanome
female *adj.*	**γυναικείο**	ghinekio
ferry	**φέρρυ-μπότ**	ferry-boat
fetch (to)	**φέρνω**	ferno
a few	**λίγα**	ligha
fiancé(e)	**αρραβωνιαστικός (-κιά)**	aravoniastikos (-kia)
field	**αγρός**	aghros
field glasses	**κυάλια**	kialia
fight (to)	**πολεμώ**	polemo
fill (to)	**γεμίζω**	ghemizo
fill in (to)	**συμπληρώνω**	simplirono
film	**φίλμ**	film
find (to)	**βρίσκω**	vrisko

fine	πρόστιμο	prostimo
finish (to)	τελειώνω	teliono
finished	τελειωμένος	teliomenos
fire	φωτιά	fotia
fire escape	έξοδος κινδύνου	eksodhos kindhinou
fire extinguisher	πυροσβεστήρας	pirosvestiras
fireworks	πυροτεχνήματα	pirotehnimata
first	πρώτος	protos
first aid	πρώτες βοήθειες	protes voithies
first class	πρώτη θέση	proti thessi
fish	ψάρι	psari
fish (to)	ψαρεύω	psarevo
fisherman	ψαράς	psaras
fit (to)	χωράω	horao
flag	σημαία	simea
flat *noun*	διαμέρισμα	dhiamerisma
flat *adj.*	επίπεδος	epipedhos
flavour	γεύση	ghefssi
flea market	παλιατζήδικο	paliadzidhiko
flight	πτήση	ptissi
float (to)	πλέω	pleo
flood	πλημμύρα	plimira
floor	πάτωμα	patoma
floor show	παράσταση	parastassi
flower	λουλούδι	louloudhi
fly	μύγα	migha

fly (to)	**πετώ**	peto
fog	**ομίχλη**	omihli
fold (to)	**διπλώνω**	dhiplono
follow (to)	**ακολουθώ**	akoloutho
food	**φαϊ**	fai
foot	**πόδι**	podhi
football	**ποδόσφαιρο**	podhosfero
footpath	**μονοπάτι**	monopati
for	**γιά**	ghia
forbid (to)	**απαγορεύω**	apaghorevo
foreign	**ξένος**	ksenos
forest	**δάσος**	dhassos
forget (to)	**ξεχνώ**	ksehno
fork	**πηρούνι**	pirouni
forward	**μπρός**	bros
fountain	**συντριβάνι**	sintrivani
fragile	**εύθραυστος**	efthrafstos
free	**ελεύθερος**	eleftheros
freight	**φορτίο**	fortio
fresh	**φρέσκος**	freskos
fresh water	**φρέσκο νερό**	fresko nero
friend	**φίλος**	filos
friendly	**φιλικός**	filikos
from	**από**	apo
front	**μπρός**	bros
frontier	**σύνορο**	sinoro

frost	παγωνιά	paghonia
frozen	παγωμένος	paghomenos
frozen food	παγωμένα (τρόφιμα)	paghomena (trofima)
fruit	φρούτο	fruto
full	γεμάτος	ghematos
full board	με όλα τα γεύματα	me ola ta ghevmata
fun	κέφι	kefi
funny	αστείος	astios
fur	γούνα	ghouna
furniture	έπιπλο	epiplo
further	παραπέρα	parapera

G

gallery	γαλαρία	ghaleria
gamble (to)	χαρτοπαίζω	hartopezo
game	παιγνίδι	peghnidhi
garage	γκαράζ	garaz
garbage	σκουπίδια	skoupidhia
garden	κήπος	kipos
gas	γκάζι	gazi
gate	πόρτα	porta
gentlemen	κύριος	kirios
genuine	γνήσιο	ghnissio
get (to)	πηγαίνω	pigheno
get off (to)	βγαίνω	vgheno
get on (to)	ανεβαίνω	aneveno

gift	**δώρο**	dhoro
gift wrap (to)	**περιτυλίγω δώρο**	peritiligho dhoro
girdle	**ζώνη**	zoni
girl	**κορίτσι**	koritsi
give (to)	**δίνω**	dhino
glad	**ευχαριστημένος**	efharistimenos
glass	**ποτήρι**	potiri
glasses	**γυαλιά**	ghialia
gloomy	**μελαγχολικός**	melanholikos
glorious	**θαυμάσιος**	thavmassios
glove	**γάντι**	ghanti
go (to)	**πηγαίνω**	pigheno
goal	**σκοπός**	skopos
god	**Θεός**	theos
gold	**χρυσός**	hrissos
gold plate	**επίχρυσο**	epihrisso
golf (course)	**γκόλφ (γήπεδον τού)**	golf (ghipedon tou)
good	**καλός**	kalos
government	**κυβέρνηση**	kivernissi
granddaughter	**εγγονή**	engoni
grandfather	**παππούς**	papous
grandmother	**γιαγιά**	ghiaghia
grandson	**εγγονός**	engonos
grass	**γρασίδι**	ghrassidhi
grateful	**ευγνώμων**	evghnomon
gravel	**χαλίκι**	haliki

great	μεγάλος	meghalos
Greece	Ελλάδα	eladha
Greek *adj*	Ελληνικός	elinikos
groceries	κομωτής	komotis
ground	έδαφος	edhafos
grow (to)	μεγαλώνω	meghalono
guarantee	εγγύηση	engiissi
guard	φρουρός	frouros
guest	φιλοξενούμενος	filoksenoumenos
guest house	ξενώνας	ksenonas
guide	οδηγός	odhighos
guide book	τουριστικός οδηγός	touristikos odhighos
guided tour	περιήγηση	periighissi

H

hair	μαλλιά	malia
hair brush	βούρτσα μαλλιών	vourtsa malion
hairdresser	κομμώτρια	komotria
hair dryer	στεγνωτήρας	steghnotiras
hair spray	σπρέϋ γιά μαλλιά	spray ghia malia
hairpin	φουρκέττα	fourketa
half	μισό	missos
half fare	μισό εισιτήριο	misso issitirio
hammer	σφυρί	sfiri
hand	χέρι	heri
handbag	τσάντα	tsanta

handkerchief	μαντήλι	mandili
handmade	χειροποίητο	hiropiito
hang (to)	κρεμώ	kremo
hanger	κρεμάστρα	kremastra
happen (to)	συμβαίνω	simveno
happy	ευτυχισμένος	eftihismenos
harbour	λιμάνι	limani
hard	σκληρός	skliros
hardly	σχεδόν καθόλου	shedhon katholou
harmless	αβλαβές	avlaves
harmful	επιβλαβές	epivlaves
hat	καπέλλο	kapelo
have (to)	έχω	eho
haversack	σακκίδιο	sakhidio
he	αυτός	aftos
head	κεφάλι	kefali
headphones	ακουστικά	akoustika
health	υγεία	ighia
hear (to)	ακούω	akouo
heart	καρδιά	kardhia
heat	ζέστη	zesti
heating	θέρμανση	thermanssi
heavy	βαρύς	varis
hedge	φράκτης	fraktis
heel *shoe*	τακούνι	takouni
height	ύψος	ipsos

helicopter	**ελικόπτερο**	elikoptero
help	**βοήθεια**	voithia
help (to)	**βοηθώ**	voitho
hem	**ποδόγυρος/στρίφωμα**	podóghiros/strifoma
her *pron.*	**αυτήν**	aftin
here	**εδώ**	edho
high	**ψηλά**	psila
hike (to)	**πεζοπορώ**	pezoporo
hill	**λόφος**	lofos
him	**αυτόν**	afton
hire (to)	**νοικιάζω**	nikiazo
his/her	**του/της**	tou/tis
history	**ιστορία**	istoria
hitchhike (to)	**κάνω ώτοστόπ**	kano otostop
hobby	**χόμπυ**	hobby
hold (to)	**κρατώ**	krato
hole	**τρύπα**	tripa
holiday	**γιορτή**	ghiorti
holidays	**γιορτές**	ghiortes
hollow *adj.*	**κούφιος**	kouffios
(at) home	**στο σπίτι**	sto spiti
honeymoon	**μήνας του μέλιτος**	minas tou melitos
hope	**ελπίδα**	elpidha
hope (to)	**ελπίζω**	elpizo
horse	**άλογο**	alogho
horse races	**ιπποδρομίες**	ipodhromies

horse riding	**καβάλα στ'άλογο**	kavala stalogho
hose	**λάστιχο**	lastiho
hospital	**νοσοκομείο**	nossokomio
host(ess)	**οικοδεσπότης/ οικοδέσποινα**	ikodhespotis/ikodhespina
hostel	**ξενώνας**	ksenonas
hot	**ζεστός**	zestos
hot water bottle	**θερμοφόρα**	thermofora
hotel	**ξενοδοχείο**	ksenodhohio
hotel keeper	**ξενοδόχος**	ksenodhohos
hour	**ώρα**	ora
house	**σπίτι**	spiti
how?	**πως;**	pos
how much, many?	**πόσα;**	possa
hungry (to be)	**πεινάω**	pinao
hunt (to)	**κυνηγώ**	kinigho
hurry (to)	**βιάζομαι**	viazome
hurt (to)	**βλάπτω**	vlapto
husband	**άνδρας, σύζυγος**	andhras, sizighos
hydrofoil	**ιπτάμενο πλοίο**	iptameno plio

I

I	**εγώ**	egho
ice	**πάγος**	paghos
ice cream	**παγωτό**	paghoto
identify (to)	**αναγνωρίζω**	anaghnorizo

if	αν	an
imagine (to)	φαντάζομαι	fantazome
immediately	αμέσως	amessos
immersion heater	ηλεκτρικος θερμοσύφωνας	ilektrikos thermossifonas
important	σπουδαίος	spoudheos
in	μέσα	messa
include (to)	συμπεριλαμβάνω	simberilamvano
included	συμπεριλαμβανόμενο	simberilamvanomeno
inconvenient	άβολος	avolos
incorrect	λανθασμένος	lanthasmenos
indeed	βεβαίως	veveos
independent	ανεξάρτητος	aneksartitos
indoors	μέσα/στο εσωτερικό	messa/sto essoteriko
industry	βιομηχανία	viomihania
inexpensive	φτηνός	ftinos
inflammable	εύφλεκτος	evflektos
inflatable	που φουσκώνει	pou fouskoni
inflation	πληθωρισμός	plithorismos
information	πληροφορία	pliroforia
information bureau	γραφείο πληροφοριών	ghrafio pliroforion
inn	χάνι	hani
insect	έντομο	endomo
insect bite	τσίμπημα από έντομο	tsimbima apo endomo

insect repellent	λοσιόν γιά την απώθηση εντόμων	lossion ghia tin apothissi entomon
inside	μέσα	messa
instead	αντί	andi
instructor	δάσκαλος	dhaskalos
insurance	ασφάλεια	asfalia
insure (to)	ασφαλίζω	asfalizo
insured	ασφαλισμένος	asfalismenos
interest *in*	ενδιαφέρον	endhiaferon
interest *on*	τόκοσ	tokos
interested	ενδιαφερόμενος	endhiaferomenos
interesting	ενδιαφέρον	endhiaferon
interpreter	μεταφραστής, διερμηνέας	metafrastis, dhiermineas
into	μέσα	messa
introduce (to)	συστήνω	sistino
invitation	πρόσκληση	prosklissi
invite (to)	προσκαλώ	proskalo
Ireland	Ιρλανδία	irlandhia
Irish	Ιρλανδός	irlandhos
iron (to)	σιδερώνω	sidherono
island	νησί	nissi
it	αυτό	afto

J

| jacket | σακκάκι | sakaki |

jar	βάζο	vazo
jelly fish	τσούχτρα	tsouhtra
Jew	Εβραίος	evreos
jewellery	κοσμήματα	kosmimata
Jewish	Εβραικός	evraikos
job	δουλειά	dhoulia
journey	ταξίδι	taksidhi
jump (to)	πηδώ	pidho
jumper	πουλόβερ	pullover

K

keep (to)	κρατώ	krato
key	κλειδί	klidhi
kick (to)	κλωτσώ	klotso
kind	είδος	idhos
kind (*adj*)	καλός	kalos
king	βασιλιάς	vassilias
kiss	φιλί	fili
kiss (to)	φιλώ	filo
kitchen	κουζίνα	kouzina
knickers/briefs	κυλότες/σώβρακα	kilotes/sovraka
knife	μαχαίρι	maheri
knock (to)	κτυπώ	ktipo
know (to) *fact*	ξέρω	ksero
know (to) *person*	γνωρίζω	ghnorizo

L

label	**ετικέττα**	etiketa
lace	**δαντέλλα**	dhantela
ladies	**κυρίες**	kiries
lake	**λίμνη**	limni
lamp	**λάμπα**	lamba
land *not sea*	**στεριά**	steria
landing *plane*	**προσγείωσις**	prosghiossis
landlady/lord	**σπιτονοικοκυρά/**	spitonikokira/
	σπιτονοικοκύρης	spitonikokiris
landmark	**ορόσημο**	orossimo
landscape	**τοπίο**	topio
lane	**δρομάκι**	dromaki
language	**γλώσσα**	ghlossa
large	**μεγάλος**	meghalos
last	**τελευταίος**	telefteos
late	**αργά**	argha
laugh (to)	**γελώ**	ghelo
launderette	**πλυντήριο ρούχων**	plintirio rouhon
lavatory	**αποχωρητήριο**	apohoritirio
law	**νόμος**	nomos
lawn	**γρασίδι**	ghrassidhi
lawyer	**δικηγόρος**	dhikighoros
lead (to)	**οδηγώ**	odhigho
leaf	**φύλλο**	filo
leak (to)	**διαρρέω**	dhiareo

learn (to)	μαθαίνω	matheno
least	λιγότερο	lighotero
leather	δέρμα	dherma
leave (to) *abandon*	εγκαταλείπω	engatalipo
leave (to) *go away*	φεύγω	fevgho
left	αριστερά	aristera
left luggage	αποσκευές	aposkeves
lend (to)	δανείζω	dhanizo
length	μήκος	mikos
less	λιγότερο	lighotero
lesson	μάθημα	mathima
let (to) *rent*	νοικιάζω	nikiazo
let (to) *allow*	επιτρέπω	epitrepo
letter	γράμμα	ghrama
level crossing	ισόπεδος διάβασις	isopedhos dhiavassis
library	βιβλιοθήκη	vivliothiki
licence	άδεια	adhia
life	ζωή	zoi
lifebelt	σωσίβιο	sossivio
lifeboat	σωσίβιος λέμβος	sossivios lemvos
lifeguard	ναυαγοσώστης	navaghossostis
lift	ασανσέρ	assanser
light *illumination*	φώς	fos
light *weight*	ελαφρύς	elafris
light meter	φωτόμετρο	fotometro
lighter fuel	βενζίνη αναπτήρος	venzini anaptiros

lighthouse	φάρος	faros
lightning	κεραυνός	keravnos
like (to) *it pleases me*	μου αρέσει	mou aressi
like (to) *wish*	θέλω	thelo
line	γραμμή	ghrami
linen	λινό	lino
lingerie	γυναικεία εσώρουχα	ghinekia essorouha
lipsalve	κρέμα γιά τα χείλια	krema ghia ta hilia
lipstick	κραγιόν	kraghion
liquid *adj.*	υγρός	ighros
liquid *noun*	υγρό	ighro
listen	ακούω	akouo
little *amount*	λίγος	lighos
little *size*	μικρός	mikros
live (to)	ζω	zo
loaf	φραντζόλα	frandzola
local	ντόπιο	dopio
lock	κλειδαριά	klidharia
lock (to)	κλειδώνω	klidhono
long	μακρύς	makris
look at (to)	βλέπω	vlepo
look for (to)	ψάχνω	psahno
look like (to)	μοιάζω	miazo
loose	χύμα	hima
lorry	φορτηγό	fortigho
lose (to)	χάνω	hano

lost property office	γραφείο χαμένων αντικειμένων	ghrafio hamenon antikimenon
lot	κλήρος	kliros
(a) lot	πολύ	poli
loud	δυνατά	dhinata
love (to)	αγαπώ	aghapo
lovely	όμορφος	omorfos
low	χαμηλός	hamilos
lucky	τυχερός	tiheros
luggage	αποσκευές	aposkeves
lunch	μεσημεριανό (φαγητό)	messimeriano (faghito)

M

mad	τρελλός	trelos
magazine	περιοδικό	periodhiko
maid	υπηρέτρια	ipiretria
mail	ταχυδρομείο	tahidhromio
main street	κύριος δρόμος	kirios dhromos
make (to)	κάνω	kano
make love (to)	κάνω έρωτα	kano erota
make-up	μακιγιάζ	makighiaz
male *adj.*	αρσενικός	arsenikos
man	άνδρας	andhras
manage (to)	καταφέρνω/διευθύνω	kataferno/dhiefthino
manager	διευθυντής	dhiefthindis

manicure	**μανικιούρ**	manikiour
man-made	**ανθρώπινο**	anthropino
many	**πολλοί**	poli
many happy returns	**χρόνια πολλά**	hronia pola
map	**χάρτης**	hartis
marble *noun*	**μάρμαρο**	marmaro
market	**αγορά**	aghora
married	**παντρεμένος**	pandremenos
marsh	**έλος**	elos
Mass	**Λειτουργία**	litourghia
massage	**μασσάζ**	massage
match	**σπίρτο**	spirto
match *sport*	**μάτζ**	match
material *cloth*	**ύφασμα**	ifasma
matinée	**απογευματινή παράσταση**	apoghevmatini parastassi
mattress	**στρώμα**	stroma
maybe	**ίσως**	issos
me	**εμένα**	emena
meal	**γεύμα**	ghevma
mean (to)	**εννοώ**	ennoö
measurements	**μέτρα**	metra
meet (to)	**συναντώ**	sinando
mend (to)	**επιδιορθώνω**	epidhiorthono
menstruation	**εμμηνόρροια**	eminoria
mess	**χάος**	haos

message	μήνυμα	minima
messenger	αγγελιοφόρος	angelioforos
metal	μέταλλο	metalo
midday	μεσημέρι	messimeri
middle	μέσος	messos
middle-aged	μεσήλιξ	messiliks
middle class	μικροαστός	mikroastos
midnight	μεσάνυχτα	messanihta
mild	ήπιος	ipios
mill	μύλος	milos
mine *pron.*	δικό μου	dhiko mou
minute	λεπτό	lepto
mirror	καθρέπτης	kathreptis
Miss	δεσποινίς	dhespinis
miss (to) *train, etc*	χάνω	hano
mistake	λάθος	lathos
mix (to)	ανακατεύω	anakatevo
mixed	ανακατεμμένος	anakatemenos
modern	μοντέρνος	modernos
moment	στιγμή	stighmi
monastery	μοναστήρι	monastiri
money	χρήματα/λεπτά	hrimata/lepta
monk	μοναχός	monahos
month	μήνας	minas
monument	μνημείο	mnimio
moon	σελήνη	selini

moorland	βαλτοτόπι	valtotopi
moped	μηχανάκι	mihanaki
more	περισσότερο	perissotero
morning	πρωί	proi
mortgage	υποθήκη	ipothiki
mosque	τζαμί	dzami
mosquito	κουνούπι	kounoupi
most	περισσότερος	perissoteros
mother	μητέρα	mitera
motor	μηχανή	mihani
motor bike	μοτοσυκλέττα	motossikleta
motor boat	βενζινάκατος	venzinakatos
motorway	αυτοκινητόδρομος	aftokinitodhromos
mountain	βουνό	vouno
mouse	ποντίκι	pondiki
mouth	στόμα	stoma
move (to)	κινούμαι	kinoume
Mr	κύριος	kirios
Mrs	κυρία	kiria
much	πολύ	poli
museum	μουσείο	moussio
music	μουσική	moussiki
must *to have to*	πρέπει	prepi
my, mine	μου, δικό μου	mou, dhiko mou
myself	εγώ ο ίδιος	egho o idhios

N

nail *finger*	νύχι	nihi
nail *as in 'hammer'*	καρφί	karfi
nail polish	βερνίκι νυχιών	verniki nihion
nailbrush	βούρτσα νυχιών	vourtsa nihion
nailfile	λίμα νυχιών	lima nihion
name	όνομα	onoma
napkin	πετσέτα	petseta
nappy	πάνα μωρού	pana morou
narrow	στενός	stenos
natural	φυσικό	fissiko
near	κοντά	konda
nearly	σχεδόν	skhedhon
necessary	αναγκαίο	anangeo
necklace	κολιέ	kolie
need (to)	χρειάζομαι	hriazome
needle	βελόνα	velona
neither	κανείς	kanis
nephew	ανεψιός	anepsios
net	δίχτυ	dhihti
never	ποτέ	pote
new	καινούργιο	kenourghio
New Zealand	Νέα Ζηλανδία	nea zilandhia
news	ειδήσεις	idhissis
newspaper	εφημερίδα	efimeridha
next	επόμενος	epomenos

nice	**συμπαθητικός**	simpathitikos
niece	**ανεψιά**	anepsia
night	**νύχτα**	nikta
nightclub	**κέντρο διασκεδάσεως**	kendro dhiaskedhasseos
nightdress	**νυκτικό**	niktiko
nobody	**κανείς**	kanis
noisy	**θορυβώδης**	thorivodhis
no	**όχι**	ohi
no one	**κανείς**	kanis
non-alcoholic	**μή αλκοολικό**	mee alkoöliko
none	**κανένας**	kanenas
normal	**φυσικός**	fissikos
north	**βορράς**	voras
nosebleed	**αίμα απ'τη μύτη**	ema apti miti
not	**δεν, μη**	dhen, mi
note	**νότα**	nota
notebook	**τετράδιο**	tetradhio
nothing	**τίποτα**	tipota
notice	**ειδοποίηση**	idhopiissi
notice (to)	**παρατηρώ**	paratiro
novel	**μυθιστόρημα**	mithistorima
now	**τώρα**	tora
number	**αριθμός**	arithmos

O

| obtain (to) | **αποκτώ** | apokto |

occasion	περίσταση	peristassi
occupation *job*	απασχόληση	apaskholissi
occupied	κατειλημμένος	katilimenos
ocean	ωκεανός	okeanos
odd *not even*	μονός	monos
odd *strange*	παράξενος	paraksenos
of	από	apo
of course	βέβαια	vevea
off *opp. on*	κλειστό	klisto
offer	προσφορά	prosfora
offer (to)	προσφέρω	prosfero
office	γραφείο	ghrafio
officer	αξιωματικός	aksiomatikos
official *noun/adj.*	επίσημος	epissimos
often	συχνά	sihna
oily	λαδερό	ladhero
ointment	αλοιφή	alifi
OK	εν τάξει	entaksi
old	γέρος, παλιός	gheros, palios
on	πάνω	pano
on foot	με τα πόδια	me ta podhia
on time	στήν ώρα	stin ora
once	μιά φορά	mia fora
only	μόνο	mono
open (to)	ανοίγω	anigho
open *pp., adj.*	ανοικτός	aniktos

open-air	έξω	ekso
opening	άνοιγμα	anighma
opera	όπερα	opera
opportunity	ευκαιρία	efkeria
opposite	αντίθετος	antithetos
optician	οφθαλμίατρος	otthalmiatros
or	ή	i
orchard	δεντρόκηπος	dhendrokipos
orchestra	ορχήστρα	orhistra
order (to)	διατάζω	dhiatazo
ordinary	συνηθισμένος	sinithismenos
orthodox	ορθόδοξος	orthodhoksos
other	άλλος	alos
otherwise	αλλοιώς	alios
ought	πρέπει	prepi
our, ours	μας, δικός μας	mas, dhikos mas
out(side)	έξω	ekso
out of order	χαλασμένο	halasmeno
(it is) out of stock	τέλειωσε	teliosse
over	από πάνω	apo pano
over there	εκεί	eki
overcoat	παλτό	palto
overnight	γιά μία μόνο νύχτα	ghia mia mono nikta
owe (to)	χρωστώ	hrosto
owner	ιδιοκτήτης	idhioktitis

P

pack (to)	πακετάρω	paketaro
packet	πακέτο	paketo
paddle	κουπί	koupi
paddling pool	πισίνα γιά μικρά παιδιά	pissina ghia mikra pedhia
page	σελίδα	selidha
paid	πληρωμένος	pliromenos
pain	πόνος	ponos
painkiller	παυσίπονο	pafsipono
paint (to)	ζωγραφίζω	zoghrafizo
painting	πίνακας ζωγραφικής	pinakas zoghrafikis
pair	ζευγάρι	zevghari
palace	παλάτι	palati
pale	χλωμός	hlomos
paper	χαρτί	harti
parcel	πακέτο	paketo
park	πάρκο	parko
park (to)	σταθμεύω	stathmevo
parking disc	δίσκος σταθμεύσεως αυτοκινήτου	dhiskos stathmefseos aftokinitou
parking meter	παρκόμετρο	parkometro
parking ticket	κλήση γιά παράνομη στάθμευση	klissi ghia paranomi stathmefsi
parliament	βουλή	vouli
part	μέρος	meros

party *political*	**κόμμα**	koma
pass (to)	**περνώ**	perno
passenger	**επιβάτης**	epivatis
passport	**διαβατήριο**	dhiavatirio
past *opp. future*	**παρελθόν**	parelthon
path	**μονοπάτι**	monopati
patient *adj.*	**υπομονετικός**	ipomonetikos
pavement	**πεζοδρόμιο**	pezodhromio
pay (to)	**πληρώνω**	plirono
payment	**πληρωμή**	pliromi
peace	**ειρήνη**	irini
peak	**κορυφή**	korifi
pearl	**πέρλα, μαργαριτάρι**	perla, margharitari
pebble	**χαλίκι**	haliki
pedal	**πεντάλι**	pedali
pedestrian	**πεζός**	pezos
pedestrian crossing	**διάβαση πεζών**	dhiavassi pezon
pedestrian precinct	**πεζόδρομος**	pezodhromos
penknife	**σουγιάς**	soughias
pensioner	**συνταξιούχος**	sintaksiouhos
people	**κόσμος**	kosmos
per person	**κατ'άτομον**	katatomon
perfect	**τέλειος**	telios
performance	**παράσταση**	parastassi
perfume	**άρωμα**	aroma
perhaps	**ίσως**	issos

perishable	φθαρτό	ftharto
permit	άδεια	adhia
permit (to)	επιτρέπω	epitrepo
person	άνθρωπος	anthropos
personal	προσωπικός	prossopikos
petrol	βενζίνη	venzini
petticoat	μεσοφόρι	messofori
photograph	φωτογραφία	fotoghrafia
photographer	φωτογράφος	fotoghrafos
piano	πιάνο	piano
pick (to)	μαζεύω	mazevo
picnic	πικνίκ	piknik
piece	κομμάτι	komati
pier	αποβάθρα	apovathra
pillow	μαξιλλάρι	maksilari
pin	καρφίτσα	karfitsa
(safety) pin	παραμάνα	paramana
pipe	πίπα	pipa
pity	κρίμα	krima
place	μέρος	meros
plain *simple*	απλός	aplos
plan	σχέδιο	skhedhio
plant	φυτό	fito
plastic	πλαστικός	plastikos
plate	πιάτο	piato
platform	εξέδρα/πλατφόρμα	eksedhra/platforma

play (to)	παίζω	pezo
player	παίχτης	pektis
please	παρακαλώ	parakalo
pleased	ευχαριστημένος	efharistimenos
plenty	αρκετός	arketos
pliers	πένσα	pensa
plimsoll	πάνινα παπούτσια	panina papoutsia
plug *bath*	βούλωμα	vouloma
plug *electric*	πρίζα	priza
pocket	τσέπη	tsepi
point *sharp end*	σημείο	simmio
poisonous	δηλητηριώδης	dhilitiriodhis
police station	αστυνομία	astinomia
policeman	αστυνόμος	astinomos
politician/political	πολιτικός	politikos
politics	πολιτικά	politika
pollution	ρύπανσις ατμόσφαιρας	ripansis atmosferas
pond	λίμνη	limni
poor	φτωχός	ftohos
pope	Πάπας	papas
popular	δημοφιλής	dhimofilis
porcelain	πορσελάνη	porselani
port	λιμάνι	limani
possible	δυνατόν	dhinaton
post (to)	ταχυδρομώ	tahidhromo

post box	γραμματοκιβώτιο	ghramatokivotio
post office	ταχυδρομείο	tahidhromio
postcard	καρτ ποστάλ	kart postal
postman	ταχυδρόμος	tahidhromos
postpone (to)	αναβάλλω	anavalo
pound	λίρα	lira
powder	σκόνη	skoni
prefer (to)	προτιμώ	protimo
pregnant	έγκυος	engios
prepare (to)	ετοιμάζω	etimazo
present *gift*	δώρο	dhoro
president	πρόεδρος	proedhros
press (to)	σιδερώνω	sidherono
pretty	όμορφη	omorfi
price	τιμή	timi
priest	παπάς	papas
prime minister	πρωθυπουργός	prothipourghos
print	γκραβούρα	gravoura
print (to)	τυπώνω	tipono
private	ιδιωτικός	idhiotikos
problem	πρόβλημα	provlima
profession	επάγγελμα	epangelma
programme	πρόγραμμα	proghramma
promise	υπόσχεση	iposkhessi
promise (to)	υπόσχομαι	iposkhome
prompt	παρακινώ	parakino

protestant	προτεστάντης	protestandis
provide (to)	προμηθεύω	promithevo
public *adj.*	δημόσιος	dhimossios
public holiday	δημόσια γιορτή	dhimossia ghiorti
pull (to)	τραβώ	travo
pump	αντλία	andlia
pure *genuine*	γνήσιο	ghnissio
purse	πορτοφόλι	portofoli
push (to)	σκουντώ	skoundo
put (to)	βάζω	vazo
pyjamas	πιτζάμες	pidzames

Q

quality	ποιότητα	piotita
quantity	ποσότητα	possotita
quarter	τέταρτο	tetarto
queen	βασίλισσα	vassilissa
question	ερώτηση	erotissi
queue	σειρά	sira
queue (to)	κάνω ουρά	kano oura
quick	γρήγορος	ghrighoros
quiet	ήσυχος	issihos
quite *fairly*	αρκετά	arketa

R

race *running*	αγώνας δρόμου	aghonas dhromou

racecourse	ιππόδρομος	ipodhromos
radiator	καλοριφέρ	kalorifer
radio	ραδιόφωνο	radhiofono
railway	σιδηρόδρομος	sidhirodhromos
rain	βροχή	vrohi
(it is) raining	βρέχει	vrehi
raincoat	αδιάβροχο	adhiavroho
rare	σπάνιος	spanios
rash *noun*	εξάνθημα	eksanthima
rate *of growth*	ρυθμός	rithmos
rather	αρκετά	arketa
raw	ωμός	omos
razor	ξυράφι	ksirafi
razor blade	ξυραφάκι	ksirafaki
reach (to) *arrive*	φθάνω	fthano
read (to)	διαβάζω	dhiavazo
ready	έτοιμος	etimos
real	πραγματικός	praghmatikos
really	πραγματικά	praghmatika
reason	λογική	loghiki
receipt	απόδειξη	apodhiksi
receive (to)	λαβαίνω	laveno
recent	πρόσφατος	prosfatos
recipe	συνταγή	sintaghi
recognize (to)	αναγνωρίζω	anaghnorizo
recommend	συστήνω	sistino

record *music*	δίσκος γραμμοφώνου	dhiskos ghramofonou
record *sport*	ρεκόρ	recor
refill *noun*	ανταλλακτικό	antalaktiko
refreshments	αναψυκτικά	anapsiktika
refrigerator	ψυγείο	psighio
refund	επιστροφή χρημάτων	epistrofi hrimaton
regards	χαιρετίσματα	heretismata
register (to)	δηλώνω	dhilono
relatives	συγγενείς	singenis
religion	θρησκεία	thriskia
remember (to)	θυμάμαι	thimame
rent	ενοίκιο	enikio
rent (to)	νοικιάζω	nikiazo
repair (to)	διορθώνω	dhiorthono
repeat (to)	επαναλαμβάνω	epanalamvano
reply (to)	απαντώ	apanto
report *noun*	αναφορά	anafora
reservation	κράτηση	kratissi
reserve (to)	κρατώ, κλείνω	krato, klino
reserved	κλεισμένο	klismeno
restaurant	εστιατόριο	estiatorio
restaurant car	βαγκόν-ρεστωράν	vakhon-restoran
return (to)	επιστρέφω	epistrefo
reward	αμοιβή	amivi
ribbon	κορδέλλα	kordhela
rich	πλούσιος	ploussios

ride *car*	βόλτα	volta
ride (to) *horse*	ιππεύω	ipevo
right *opp. left*	δεξιός	dheksios
right *opp. wrong*	ορθός, σωστός	orthos, sostos
ring	δακτυλίδι	dhaktilidhi
ripe	ώριμος	orimos
rise (to) *get up*	σηκώνομαι	sikonome
river	ποταμός	potamos
road	δρόμος	dhromos
road map	οδικός χάρτης	odhikos hartis
road sign	οδική πινακίδα	odhiki pinakidha
road works	οδικά έργα	odhika ergha
rock	βράχος	vrahos
roll (to)	κυλώ/κουλουριάζω	kilo/koulouriazo
rollers *hair*	μπικουτί	bikouti
roof	σκεπή	skepi
room	δωμάτιο	dhomatio
rope	σκοινί	skini
rotten	σάπιος	sapios
rough *texture*	αδρός	adhros
round	γύρω	ghiro
rowing boat	βάρκα με κουπιά	varka me koupia
rubber	λάστιχο	lastiho
rubbish	σκουπίδια	skoupidhia
rucksack	σακκίδιο	sakidhio
rude	αγενής	aghenis

ruin	**ερείπιο**	eripio
ruins	**ερείπια**	eripia
rule (to)	**κυβερνώ**	kiverno
run (to)	**τρέχω**	treho

S

sad	**λυπημένος**	lipimenos
saddle	**σέλλα**	sela
safe	**ασφαλής**	asfalis
sail	**πανί**	pani
sailing boat	**ιστιοφόρο**	istioforo
sailor	**ναύτης**	naftis
sale *clearance*	**ξεπούλημα**	ksepoulima
(for) sale	**προς πώλησιν**	pros polissin
salesgirl	**πωλήτρια**	politria
salesman	**πωλητής**	politis
salt	**αλάτι**	alati
salt water	**αλμυρό νερό**	almiro nero
same	**ίδιος**	idhios
sand	**άμμος**	amos
sandals	**σανδάλια**	sandhalia
sanitary towel	**πετσέτα υγείας**	petseta ighias
satisfactory	**ικανοποιητικός**	ikanopiitikos
saucer	**πιατάκι**	piataki
save (to)	**σώζω**	sozo
say (to)	**λέω**	leo

cald (to)	ζεματίζω	zematizo
carf	σάλι	sali
cenery	θέα	thea
cent	άρωμα	aroma
chool	σχολείο	skholio
cissors	ψαλίδι	psalidhi
Scotland	Σκωτία	skotia
Scottish	Σκωτσέζικο	skotseziko
cratch (to)	γρατσουνίζω	ghradzounizo
crew	βίδα	vidha
crewdriver	κατσαβίδι	katsavidhi
culpture	γλυπτική	ghliptiki
ea	θάλασσα	thalassa
ea food	ψαρικά	psarika
easick (to be)	έχω ναυτία	eho naftia
eason	εποχή	epohi
eat	θέση	thessi
eat belt	ζώνη ασφαλείας	zoni asfalias
econd hand	μεταχειρισμένο	metahirismeno
ecretary	γραμματέας	ghramateas
ee (to)	βλέπω	vlepo
eem (to)	φαίνομαι	fenome
elf-catering	αυτοεξυπηρέτηση	aftoeksipiretissi
elf-contained	αυτεξούσιο	afteksoussio
ell (to)	πουλώ	poulo
end (to)	στέλνω	stelno

separate	χωριστός	horistos
serious	σοβαρός	sovaros
serve (to)	σερβίρω	serviro
service	υπηρεσία	ipiressia
service *church*	λειτουργία	litourghia
several	αρκετός	arketos
sew (to)	ράβω	ravo
shade *colour*	απόχρωση	apohrossi
shade *shadow*	σκιά	skia
shallow	ρηχός	rihos
shampoo	σαμπουάν	sampouan
shape	σχήμα	skhima
share (to)	μοιράζομαι	mirazome
sharp	οξύς, κοφτερός	oksis, kofteros
shave (to)	ξυρίζομαι	ksirizome
shaving brush	βούρτσα ξυρίσματος	vourtsa ksirismatos
shaving cream	κρέμα ξυρίσματος	krema ksirismatos
she	αυτή	afti
sheet	σεντόνι	sendoni
shelf	ράφι	rafi
shell	κέλυφος, κοχύλι	kelifos, kohili
shelter	καταφύγειο	katafighio
shine (to)	γυαλίζω	ghializo
shingle	βότσαλο	votsalo
ship	καράβι, πλοίο	karavi, plio
shipping line	ναυτιλιακή γραμμή	naftiliaki ghrami

hirt	πουκάμισο	poukamisso
hock	κλονισμός	klonismos
hoe	παπούτσι	papoutsi
hoe polish	βερνίκι γιά παπούτσια	verniki ghia papoutsia
hoelace	κορδόνι παπουτσιών	kordhoni papoutsion
hop	κατάστημα, μαγαζί	katastima, maghazi
hopping centre	αγορά	aghora
hore	παραλία	paralia
hort	κοντός	kondos
hortly	σύντομα	sintoma
houlder	ώμος	omos
how	παράσταση	parastassi
how (to)	δείχνω	dhihno
hower	ντους	douz
hut (to)	κλείνω	klino
ide	πλευρά	plevra
ights	αξιοθέατα	aksiotheata
ightseeing	επίσκεψη των αξιοθεάτων/ περιήγηση	episkepsi ton aksiotheaton/periighissi
ign	πινακίδα	pinakidha
ign (to)	υπογράφω	ipoghrafo
ignpost	πινακίς τροχαίας	pinakis troheas
ilver	ασημένιος	assimenios
imple	απλός	aplos
nce	από τότε	apo tote

sing (to)	τραγουδώ	traghoudho
single	μονός	monos
single room	μονό δωμάτιο	mono dhomatio
sister	αδελφή	adhelfi
sit (to)	κάθομαι	kathome
sit down (to)	κάθομαι κάτω	kathome kato
size	μέγεθος	meghethos
ski (to)	κάνω σκι	kano ski
skid (to)	γλιστρώ	ghlistro
skirt	φούστα	fousta
sky	ουρανός	ouranos
sleep (to)	κοιμάμαι	kimame
sleeper	βαγκόν-λί	vakhon-li
sleeping bag	σάκκος ύπνου	sakkos ipnou
sleeve	μανίκι	maniki
slice	φέτα	feta
slippers	παντόφλες	pandofles
slowly	αργά	argha
small	μικρός	mikros
smart	κομψός	kompsos
smell	μυρωδιά	mirodhia
smell (to)	μυρίζω	mirizo
smile (to)	χαμογελώ	hamoghelo
smoke (to)	καπνίζω	kapnizo
smoking (compartment)	καπνιστήριο	kapnistirio

(no) smoking	απαγορεύεται το κάπνισμα	apaghorevete to kapnisma
snack	μεζές	mezes
snorkel	αναπνευστήρας	anapnevstiras
snow	χιόνι	hioni
(it is) snowing	χιονίζει	hionizi
so	έτσι	etsi
soap	σαπούνι	sapouni
soap powder	σκόνη σαπουνιού	skoni sapouniou
sober	σοβαρός	sovaros
sock	κάλτσα	kaltsa
soft	μαλακός	malakos
sold	πουλημένο	poulimeno
sold out	ξεπουλημένο	ksepoulimeno
sole *shoe*	σόλα	sola
solid	στερεός	stereos
some	λίγο	ligho
somebody	κάποιος	kapios
somehow	κάπως	kapos
something	κάτι	kati
sometimes	μερικές φορές	merikes fores
somewhere	κάπου	kapou
son	γιός	ghios
song	τραγούδι	traghoudhi
soon	γρήγορα	ghrighora
sort	είδος	idhos

sound *noun*	ήχος	ihos
sound and light show	ήχος και φως	ihos ke fos
sour	ξινός	ksinos
south	νότος	notos
souvenir	ενθύμιο	enthimio
space *room*	χώρος	horos
spanner	κλειδί	klidhi
spare	εφεδρικός	efedhrikos
speak (to)	μιλάω	milao
speciality	ειδικότητα	idhikotita
spectacles	γυαλιά	ghialia
speed	ταχύτητα	tahitita
speed limit	όριον ταχύτητος	orion tahititos
spend (to)	ξοδεύω	ksodhevo
spice	μπαχαρικό	bahariko
spoon	κουτάλι	koutali
sport	σπόρ	spor
sprain (to)	στραμπουλίζω	stramboulizo
spring *mechanism*	ελατήριο	elatirio
spring *season*	άνοιξη	aniksi
spring *water*	πηγή	pighi
square *shape*	τετράγωνος	tetraghonos
square *in city*	πλατεία	platia
stables	σταύλοι	stavli
stage *theatre*	σκηνή	skini
stain	λεκές	lekes

stained	λεκιασμένος	lekiasmenos
stairs	σκάλες	skales
stale	μπαγιάτικος	baghiatikos
stalls	πλατεία	platia
stamp	γραμματόσημο	ghramatossimo
stand (to)	στέκομαι	stekome
star	άστρο	astro
start (to) *begin*	αρχίζω	arhizo
station	σταθμός	stathmos
statue	άγαλμα	aghalma
stay (to)	μένω	meno
step	βήμα	vima
steward(ess)	συνοδός	sinodhos
stick	κλωνάρι	klonari
stiff	άκαμπτος	akamptos
still *not moving*	ακίνητος	akinitos
still *time*	ακόμα	akoma
sting	τσιμπώ	tsimbo
stocking	κάλτσα	kaltsa
stolen	κλεμμένο	klemeno
stone	πέτρα	petra
stool	σκαμνί	skamni
stop (to)	σταματώ	stamato
store *shop*	κατάστημα	katastima
storm	καταιγίδα	kateghidha
stove	θερμάστρα	thermastra

straight	ίσια	issia
straight on	ίσια μπρός	issia bros
strange *not familiar*	παράξενος	paraksenos
strap	λουρί	louri
stream	ρυάκι	riaki
street	δρόμος	dhromos
street map	οδικός χάρτης	odhikos hartis
streetcar	λεωφορείο	leoforio
stretch (to)	τεντώνω	tendono
string	σπάγγος	spangos
strong	δυνατός	dhinatos
student	μαθητής, φοιτητής	mathitis, fititis
stung (to be)	τσιμπημένος	tsimbimenos
style	στυλ	stil
subject	υποκείμενο	ipokimeno
suburb	περίχωρο	perihoro
subway	υπόγειος	ipoghios
such	τέτοιος	tetios
suddenly	ξαφνικά	ksafnika
suede	σουέντ	souëd
sugar	ζάχαρη	zahari
suggestion	πρόταση	protassi
suit	κοστούμι	kostoumi
suitcase	βαλίτσα	valitsa
summer	καλοκαίρι	kalokeri
sun	ήλιος	ilios

sunbathing	ηλιοθεραπεία	iliotherapia
sunburn	ηλιόκαμα	iliokama
sunglasses	γυαλιά ηλίου	ghialia iliou
sunhat	καπέλλο ηλίου	kapelo iliou
sunrise	ανατολή	anatoli
sunshade	ομπρέλλα ηλίου	ombrella iliou
suntan cream	κρέμα ηλίου	krema iliou
supper	δείπνο	dhipno
sure	βέβαιος	veveos
surfboard	σανίδα κολυμπίσεως	sanida kolimbiseos
surgery	ιατρείο	iatrio
surprise	έκπληξη	ekpliksi
surprise (to)	εκπλήσσω	ekpliso
surroundings	περίχωρα	perihora
sweat	ιδρώτας	idhrotas
sweater	πουλόβερ	pullover
sweet	γλυκός	ghlikos
sweets	γλυκά	ghlika
swell (to)	πρήζομαι	prizome
swim (to)	κολυμπώ	kolimbo
swimming pool	πισίνα	pissina
swings	κούνιες	kounies
switch *light*	διακόπτης	dhiakoptis
swollen	πρησμένος	prismenos
synagogue	συναγωγή	sinaghoghi

T

table	τραπέζι	trapezi
tablecloth	τραπεζομάντηλο	trapezomandilo
tablet	χάπι	hapi
tailor	ράφτης	raftis
take (to)	παίρνω	perno
talk (to)	μιλάω	milao
tall	ψηλός	psilos
tampon	ταμπόν	tampon
tank *reservoir*	ντεπόζιτο	depozito
tanned	μαυρισμένος	mavrismenos
tap	βρύση	vrissi
tapestry	τάπης τοίχου	tapis tihou
taste	γεύση	ghefsi
taste (to)	γεύομαι	ghevome
tax	φόρος	foros
taxi	ταξί	taksi
taxi rank	σταθμός γιά ταξί	stathmos ghia taksi
teach (to)	διδάσκω	dhidhasko
tear *torn*	σκίσιμο	skissimo
tear (to)	σκίζω	skizo
teaspoon	κουτάλι του γλυκού	koutali tou ghlikou
telephone	τηλέφωνο	tilefono
telephone (to)	τηλεφωνώ	tilefono
telephone box	τηλεφωνικός θάλαμος	tilefonikos thalamos

telephone call	τηλεφώνημα	tilefonima
television	τηλεόραση	tileorassi
telex	τέλεξ	teleks
tell (to)	λέω	leo
temperature *heat*	θερμοκρασία	thermokrassia
temple	ναός	naos
temporary	προσωρινός	prossorinos
tennis	τεννις	tennis
tent	τέντα, σκηνή	tenda, skini
tent peg	παλούκι τέντας	palouki tendas
tent pole	πάσσαλος τέντας	passalos tendas
terrace	ταράτσα	taratsa
than	από	apo
thank you	ευχαριστώ	efharisto
that	εκείνο	ekino
the	το	to
theatre	θέατρο	theatro
their, theirs	τους, δικό τους	tous, dhiko tous
them	αυτούς	aftous
then	τότε	tote
there	εκεί	eki
there is/are	είναι	ine
thermometer	θερμόμετρο	thermometro
these	αυτά	afta
they	αυτοί	afti
thick *liquid*	πηκτός	piktos

thief	**κλέφτης**	kleftis
thin *fine*	**λεπτό**	lepto
thing	**πράγμα**	praghma
think (to)	**σκέπτομαι**	skeptome
thirsty (to be)	**διψάω**	dhipsao
this	**αυτό**	afto
those	**εκείνα**	ekina
though	**αν και**	an ke
thread	**κλωστή**	klosti
through	**διά**	dhia
throughout	**παντού**	pantou
throw (to)	**πετώ**	peto
thunder	**βροντή**	vrondi
thunderstorm	**καταιγίδα με κεραυνούς**	kateghidha me keravnous
ticket	**εισιτήριο**	issitirio
ticket office	**γραφείο εισιτηρίων**	ghrafio issitirion
tide	**παλίρροια**	paliria
tie *clothing*	**γραβάτα**	ghravata
tie *sport*	**ισοπαλία**	issopalia
tight	**στενός**	stenos
tights	**καλσόν**	kalson
time	**ώρα**	ora
timetable	**ωράριο**	orario
tin can	**κονσέρβα**	konserva
tin opener	**ανοικτήρι κονσερβών**	aniktiri konservon

tip *gratuity*	πουρμπουάρ	pourbouar
tip *point*	άκρη	akri
tip (to)	δίνω φιλοδώρημα	dhino filodhorima
tired	κουρασμένος	kourasmenos
tissues *paper*	χαρτομάντηλα	hartomandila
to *place masc., fem., neut.*	στον, στη, στο	ston, sti, sto
tobacco	καπνός	kapnos
tobacco pouch	καπνοσακκούλα	kapnosakoula
today	σήμερα	simera
together	μαζί	mazi
toilet	τουαλέτα, αποχωρητήριο	toualeta, apohoritirio
toilet paper	χαρτί αποχωρητηρίου	harti apohoritiriou
token *telephone*	μάρκα	marka
toll	διόδια	dhiodhia
tomorrow	αύριο	avrio
tonight	απόψε	apopse
too *excessive*	πάρα πολύ	para poli
too *also*	επίσης καί	epissis ke
too much/many	πάρα πολύ/πάρα πολλά	para poli/para pola
toothbrush	οδοντόβουρτσα	odhondovourtsa
toothpaste	οδοντόπαστα	odhondopasta
toothpick	οδοντογλυφίδα	odhondoghlifidha
top	κορφή	korfi

torch	δαυλός	dhavlos
torn	σκισμένος	skismenos
touch (to)	ακουμπώ	akoumbo
tough	γερός	gheros
tour	τούρ	tour
tourist	επισκέπτης, τουρίστας	episkeptis, touristas
tourist office	τουριστικό γραφείο	touristiko ghrafio
towards	προς	pros
towel	πετσέτα	petseta
tower	πύργος	pirghos
town	πόλη	poli
town hall	δημαρχείο	dhimarhio
toy	παιγνίδι	peghnidhi
traffic	κυκλοφορία	kikloforia
traffic jam	κυκλοφοριακός συνωστισμός	kikloforiakos sinostismos
traffic lights	κυκλοφοριακά φώτα	kikloforiaka fota
trailer	ρυμουλκούμενο όχημα	rimoulkoumeno ohima
train	τραίνο	treno
transfer (to)	μεταφέρομαι	metaferome
transit	τράνζιτο	tranzito
translate (to)	μεταφράζω	metafrazo
travel (to)	ταξιδεύω	taksidhevo
travel agent	ταξιδιωτικό γραφείο	taksidhiotiko ghrafio
traveller	ταξιδιώτης	taksidhiotis

travellers' cheque	τράβελλερς τσέκ	travellers' cheque
treat (to) *manner*	μεταχειρίζομαι	metahirizome
treatment *manner*	τρόπος μεταχειρίσεως	tropos metahirisseos
treatment *for illness*	θεραπεία	therapia
tree	δέντρο	dhendtro
trip	ταξίδι	taksidhi
trouble *annoyance*	ενόχληση	enohlissi
trouble *worry*	ανησυχία	anissihia
trouble *cause fuss*	ταραχή	tarahi
trousers	πανταλόνια	pandalonia
true	αληθινός	alithinos
trunk *luggage*	μπαούλο	baoulo
trunks	μαγιό	maghio
truth	αλήθεια	alithia
try (to) *attempt*	προσπαθώ	prospatho
try on (to)	δοκιμάζω	dhokimazo
tunnel	σήραγξ/τούνελ	siranks/tounel
turn (to)	γυρνώ	ghirno
turning	γύρισμα, στροφή	ghirisma, strofi
tweezers	τσιμπιδάκι	tsimbidhaki
twilight	σούρουπο	souroupo
twin beds	δύο κρεββάτια πλάι πλάι	dhio krevatia plai plai
twisted	στριμμένος	strimenos
typewriter	γραφομηχανή	ghrafomihani

U

ugly	**άσχημος**	askimos
umbrella	**ομπρελλα**	ombrella
uncle	**θείος**	thios
uncomfortable	**στενόχωρος**	stenohoros
unconscious	**αναίσθητος**	anesthitos
under	**από κάτω**	apo kato
underground	**υπόγειος**	ipoghios
underneath	**από κάτω**	apo kato
understand	**καταλαβαίνω**	katalaveno
underwater fishing	**υποβρύχιο ψάρεμμα**	ipovrihio psarema
underwear	**εσώρουχα**	essorouha
university	**πανεπιστήμιο**	panepistimio
unpack (to)	**ξετυλίγω**	ksetiligho
until	**μέχρισέως ότου**	mehriseos otou
unusual	**ασυνήθης**	assinithis
up	**πάνω**	pano
upstairs	**επάνω**	epano
urgent	**επείγον**	epighon
us	**εμάς**	emas
use (to)	**χρησιμοποιώ**	hrissimopio
useful	**χρήσιμο**	hrissimo
useless	**άχρηστο**	ahristo
usual	**συνήθης**	sinithis
USA	**Ηνωμένες Πολιτείες Αμερικής – ΗΠΑ**	inomenes polities amerikis – ita pi alfa

V

vacancies	κενές θέσεις	kenes thessis
vacant	ελεύθερος	eleftheros
valid	ισχύων	ishion
valley	κοιλάδα	kiladha
valuable	πολύτιμος	politimos
value	αξία	aksia
vase	βάζο	vazo
VAT	φόρος πωλήσεως/ πληρώσωφόρο	foros polisseos/ plirossoforo
vegetables	λαχανικά	lahanika
vegetarian	χορτοφάγος	hortofaghos
vein	φλέβα	fleva
velvet	βελούδο	veloudho
ventilation	εξαερισμός	eksaerismos
very	πολύ	poli
very little	πολύ λίγο	poli ligho
very much	πάρα πολύ	para poli
video cassette	βιντεοκασσέττα	videokasseta
video recorder	βίντεο	video
view	θέα	thea
villa	βίλλα	villa
village	χωριό	horio
vineyard	αμπελώνας	ambelonas
violin	βιολί	violi
visa	βίζα	viza

visibility	**ορατότης**	oratotis
visit	**επίσκεψη**	episkepsi
visit (to)	**επισκέπτομαι**	episkeptome
voice	**φωνή**	foni
voltage	**βολτάζ**	voltaz
voucher	**κουπόνι**	kouponi
voyage	**ταξίδι**	taksidhi

W

wait (to)	**περιμένω**	perimeno
waiter	**σερβιτόρος**	servitoros
waiting room	**αίθουσα αναμονής**	ethoussa anamonis
waitress	**σερβιτόρα**	servitora
wake (to)	**ξυπνώ**	ksipno
Wales	**Ουαλία**	oualia
walk	**περίπατος**	peripatos
walk (to)	**περπατώ**	perpato
wall	**τοίχος**	tihos
wall plug	**πρίζα**	priza
wallet	**πορτοφόλι**	portofoli
want (to)	**θέλω**	thelo
wardrobe	**γκαρνταρόμπα**	gardaroba
warm/lukewarm	**ζεστός/χλιαρός**	zestos/hliaros
wash (to)	**πλένω**	pleno
washbasin	**νυπτήρας**	niptiras
waste	**απορρίμματα**	aporimata

waste (to)	σπαταλώ	spatalo
watch	ρολόϊ	roloï
water (fresh, salt)	νερό (γλυκό, θαλασσινό)	nero (ghliko, thalassino)
water skiing	θαλάσσιο σκι	thalassio ski
waterfall	καταρράκτης	kataraktis
waterproof	αδιάβροχος	adhiavrohos
wave *sea*	κύμα	kima
way	δρόμος	dhromos
we	εμείς	emis
wear (to)	φορώ	foro
weather	καιρός	keros
weather forecast	πρόβλεψη καιρού	provlepsi kerou
wedding ring	βέρα	vera
week	εβδομάδα	evdhomadha
weigh (to)	ζυγίζω	zighizo
weight	βάρος	varos
welcome *reception*	υποδοχή	ipodhohi
welcome!	καλως ορίσατε!	kalos orissate!
well	καλά	kala
well *water*	πηγάδι	pighadhi
Welshman	Ουαλός	oualos
west	δύση	dhissi
wet	βρεμμένος	vremenos
what?	τί;	ti
wheel	ρόδα, τροχός	rodha, trohos

wheelchair	**καρρότσι αναπήρου**	karotsi anapirou
when?	**πότε;**	pote
where?	**που;**	pou
whether	**κατά πόσον**	kata posson
which?	**ποιό;**	pio
while	**κατά τη διάρκεια**	kata ti dhiarkia
who?	**ποιός;**	pios
whole	**ολόκληρος**	olokliros
whose?	**ποιού, ποιανού;**	piou, pianou
why?	**γιατί;**	ghiati
wide	**πλατύς**	platis
widow/widower	**χήρα/χήρος**	hira/hiros
wife	**γυναίκα, σύζυγος**	ghineka, sizighos
wild	**άγριος**	aghrios
win (to)	**κερδίζω νικώ**	kerdhizo niko
wind	**αέρας**	aeras
window	**παράθυρο**	parathiro
wine merchant	**έμπορος κρασιών**	emboros krassion
wing	**φτερούγα**	fterougha
winter	**χειμώνας**	himonas
winter sports	**χειμερινά σπορ**	himerina spor
wire	**σύρμα**	sirma
wish (to)	**θέλω**	thelo
with	**με**	me
within	**μέσα**	messa
without	**χωρίς**	horis

witness	μάρτυρας	martiras
woman	γυναίκα	ghineka
wonderful	θαυμάσιος	thavmassios
wood	ξύλο	ksilo
wool	μαλλί	mali
word	λέξη	leksi
work	δουλειά	dhoulia
work (to)	δουλεύω	dhoulevo
worry (to)	ανησυχώ	anissiho
world	κόσμος	kosmos
worse	χειρότερος	hiroteros
worth (to be)	αξίζω	aksizo
wrap (to)	τυλίγω	tiligho
write (to)	γράφω	ghrafo
wrong	λανθασμένος	lanthasmenos

X

| xerox | φωτοτυπία | fototipia |
| X-ray | ακτινογραφία | aktinoghrafia |

Y

yacht	γιώτ	ghiot
year	χρόνος	hronos
yes	ναί	ne
yesterday	χθές	hthes
yet	ακόμα	akoma

you	εσύ	essi
young	νέος	neos
your, yours	σου, δικό σου	sou, dhiko sou
youth hostel	ξενώνας νεότητος	ksenonas neotitos

Z

| zip | φερμουάρ | fermouar |
| zoo | ζωολογικός κήπος | zoologhikos kipos |

INDEX

NOTES

NOTES